Table of Contents

Frank Schaffer Publications®

Send all inquiries to:
Frank Schaffer Publications
3195 Wilson Drive NW
Grand Rapids, Michigan 49534

Reading—Grade 3

ISBN 0-7696-8233-2

1 2 3 4 5 6 7 8 9 10 WAL 10 09 08 07 06

Review Consonant Digraphs

Remember, a consonant digraph is two or three letters together that make one sound.

Directions: Write the letter of the word that best completes the sentence.

a. knew	**e.** thorny	**i.** chest	**m.** wrote
b. thermos	**f.** beneath	**j.** bush	**n.** shovel
c. where	**g.** think	**k.** wrong	
d. character	**h.** showed	**l.** crunch	

1. I _____ a story about a search for hidden riches.

2. The main _____ was a man who searched for buried treasure.

3. He walked for miles and drank water from a _____.

4. The map he used _____ an oddly shaped rock.

5. He found the rock and reached _____ it.

6. Somehow, he _____ that nothing would be there.

7. He thought about _____ he could look next.

8. He noticed a green _____ growing nearby.

9. The explorer shoved its _____ branches aside.

10. Then, he reached for a _____ and began to dig.

11. After digging for awhile, he heard a loud _____.

12. The sound made him _____ he had hit a rock.

13. He was definitely _____!

14. It was a _____ filled with shiny jewels and gold.

3

Vowel Digraphs

A **vowel digraph** is two vowels together that make one sound. The vowel digraphs **ei** and **ey** can have the sound of long **a** or long **e**.

Examples: long a sound
       ei in **ei**ght
       ey in th**ey**

       long e sound
       ei in c**ei**ling
       ey in monk**ey**

Directions: Write long **a** or long **e** for the sound of the vowel digraph in each underlined word.

1. The people next door are my <u>neighbors</u>. _____

2. <u>They</u> are very friendly. _____

3. The son is <u>eighteen</u> years old. _____

4. They made us a <u>turkey</u> on Thanksgiving Day. _____

5. I learned that a turkey is not a bird of <u>prey</u>. _____

6. Once we lost the <u>key</u> to our front door. _____

7. We paid <u>money</u> to have the door opened. _____

8. The locksmith gave my dad a <u>receipt</u> for it. _____

9. That week, Dad also had to fix the <u>ceiling</u>. _____

10. He spent a total of <u>eighty</u> dollars. _____

11. Dad earns money by loading <u>freight</u> at work. _____

12. A shipment of <u>sleighs</u> came in last week. _____

13. Dad had to <u>survey</u> the large boxes. _____

14. The <u>weight</u> of the shipment was very heavy. _____

The Tie Thief

The vowel digraph **ie** can have the sound of long **i** or long **e**.

Examples: long i sound
    ie in t**ie**

    long e sound
    ie in th**ie**f

Directions: Write long **i** or long **e** for the sound of the vowel digraph in each underlined word.

1. The <u>chief</u> of police was called. _____

2. A thief took <u>ties</u> from Neil's closet! _____

3. Neil and his <u>niece</u> are afraid he may return. _____

4. This event caused a lot of <u>grief</u>. _____

5. The thief <u>pried</u> open the door. _____

6. Neil tried to catch him, but the <u>thief</u> was too fast. _____

7. He ran across a <u>field</u> into the woods. _____

8. Is this the only crime he ever <u>tried</u>? _____

9. I told my friend <u>Frieda</u> about the crime. _____

10. The tie thief is a terrible <u>fiend</u>. _____

11. The police found a <u>piece</u> of evidence. _____

12. They retrieved his <u>handkerchiefs</u> at the scene. _____

13. They <u>believe</u> it will help them jail the thief. _____

14. The thief didn't <u>achieve</u> much by stealing. _____

Blue Suitcase

The vowel digraphs **ue** and **ui** often have the sound of long **u**, but not always.

Examples: long u sound
ui in s**ui**tcase
ue in bl**ue**

short i sound
ui as in b**ui**lding

Directions: Write the word that has the same vowel sound as the first word in each row.

1.	**clue**	fruit	build	_____
2.	**true**	built	hue	_____
3.	**juice**	guilty	true	_____
4.	**fuel**	guild	duel	_____
5.	**glue**	building	juice	_____
6.	**build**	blue	guilt	_____

Directions: Write the word from the box that best completes each sentence.

suitable	glue	clue	due	true

1. The library sent a notice saying a fine was _____.

2. They claimed I spilled _____ on the book's pages.

3. The book is no longer _____ for reading.

4. I will pay the fine if their claim is _____.

5. I don't have a _____ about how this happened!

Name_____

Vowel Digraph ea

The vowel digraph **ea** can have the sound of short **e**, long **a**, or long **e**.

Examples: short e sound
   ea in br**ea**d

 The has the sound of short **e**.

long a sound
   ea in br**ea**k

 The has the sound of long **a**.

long e sound
   ea in s**ea**t

The has the sound of long **e**.

Directions: Write a word from the box that rhymes with the underlined word.

dread	beak	beast	steak	bread	meat
steady	preacher	mean	seal	break	disease

1. I enjoyed the characters in the book I just <u>read</u>. _____

2. My friend says the characters and events are <u>real</u>. _____

3. Let's ask the <u>teacher</u> if this is true. _____

4. We can ask her after the lunch <u>break</u>. _____

5. I hope the cafeteria serves something good to <u>eat</u>. _____

6. I feel like eating a huge <u>feast</u>. _____

7. I like when the meat in the burgers is <u>lean</u>. _____

8. Do you wish they would serve <u>steak</u> and potatoes? _____

9. Are you <u>ready</u> to eat lunch now? _____

10. I see our teacher at the <u>head</u> of the lunch line. _____

11. Would you <u>please</u> talk to the teacher for me? _____

12. Maybe we can <u>speak</u> to her after school instead. _____

Good Food

The vowel digraph **oo** can have the sound you hear in g**oo**d or f**oo**d.

Examples: c**oo**k

spoon

Directions: Write the words from the box under the correct heading.

snooze	book	room	shook
hood	stoop	stood	wool
tooth	took	foot	rooster
loose	droop	crook	proof
cookies	bloom	spool	look

Sound of **oo** as in g**oo**d   Sound of **oo** as in f**oo**d

1. _____   11. _____

2. _____   12. _____

3. _____   13. _____

4. _____   14. _____

5. _____   15. _____

6. _____   16. _____

7. _____   17. _____

8. _____   18. _____

9. _____   19. _____

10. _____   20. _____

Vowel Digraphs au and aw

The vowel digraphs **au** and **aw** usually have the same sound.

Examples: au
     s**au**ce

    aw
     j**aw**

Directions: Write the correct spelling of the word in parentheses.

1. Our summer vacation usually ends in (August, Awgust). _____

2. I love summer (because, becawse) it is a time to relax. _____

3. We have the greenest (laun, lawn) on the street. _____

4. We sip lemonade through a (strau, straw). _____

5. I read books written by my favorite (author, awthor). _____

6. My neighbor speaks with a southern (draul, drawl). _____

7. His daughter has just learned how to (crawl, craul). _____

8. They were recently (cawt, caught) in a traffic jam. _____

9. Each driver drove with (cawtion, caution). _____

10. I had just washed a load of (laundry, lawndry). _____

11. My cat (sprauled, sprawled) out on the clean clothes. _____

12. The lazy cat looked at us and (yauned, yawned). _____

13. We chased the (nawty, naughty) cat away. _____

14. The clothes were soiled from its dirty (pause, paws). _____

Diphthongs

Diphthongs are two vowels together that make a new sound.

Examples: oi
     c**oi**n

     oy
     b**oy**

     ew
     n**ew**

Directions: Write the word that has the same vowel sound as the first word in the row.

1.	**join**	turmoil	fowl	few	_____
2.	**toy**	loyal	lone	town	_____
3.	**voice**	dove	vase	annoy	_____
4.	**flew**	well	newspaper	crow	_____
5.	**coil**	clean	enjoy	clue	_____
6.	**decoy**	drew	dawn	royal	_____
7.	**renew**	stew	coin	glow	_____
8.	**loyal**	low	soil	towel	_____
9.	**employ**	power	join	umpire	_____
10.	**moist**	jewel	just	joy	_____
11.	**review**	choice	avoid	chew	_____
12.	**threw**	throw	view	toy	_____
13.	**void**	oyster	due	vendor	_____
14.	**knew**	crew	know	annoy	_____

Out, Now, Brown Cow!

Remember, diphthongs are two vowels together that make a new sound. The diphthongs **ou** and **ow** often have the same sound.

Examples: **ou**
        h**ou**se

        ow
        fl**ow**ers

Directions: Write the letters **ou** or **ow** to make a word that completes each sentence.

1. A brown c_____ was found outside my house!

2. The cow was standing near the pl_____.

3. I yelled at the animal to get _____t!

4. Suddenly, the cow turned ar_____nd.

5. I f_____nd it was heading my way.

6. The cow trampled the pretty fl_____ers.

7. I didn't know h_____ to stop it.

8. A friend I know from across t_____n helped me.

9. He told me to give a loud h_____l to distract the cow.

10. I gave him a v_____ that I would try his suggestion.

11. The s_____nd of my howl scared the cow.

12. It had the p_____er to chase it from my yard.

13. Now I d_____bt I will ever have that problem again.

14. The cow was out and b_____nd for the pasture.

    11   *Reading: Grade 3*

Compound Words

Some words are made by putting two different words together. The new word is called a **compound word.**

Example: grape + fruit = grapefruit

Directions: Draw a line to match a word from each column to make a compound word. Write each compound word on a line below.

1. high	shine
2. rail	work
3. home	boat
4. pea	way
5. sun	nut
6. base	road
7. sail	walk
8. side	brush
9. play	ball
10. tooth	ground

_____   _____

_____   _____

_____   _____

_____   _____

_____   _____

Contractions

Contractions are two words joined into one. When the words are joined, at least one letter is left out. An apostrophe replaces the missing letter or letters.

Examples:

I + will	I'll
they + are	they're
they + have	they've
has + not	hasn't
he + would	he'd

Directions: Write a contraction for each pair of words.

1. is not

_____

2. she is

_____

3. they have

_____

4. he is

_____

5. I would

_____

6. you are

_____

7. she will

_____

8. did not

_____

9. he will

_____

10. where is

_____

11. they would

_____

12. she has

_____

What's Missing?

Directions: Write the correct contraction on the line.

they're
it's
she'll
let's
we're
we'll
you're
I'm
that's
I'll
he's
they'll

1. they will _____   7. I will _____

2. that is _____   8. I am _____

3. we are _____   9. she will _____

4. let us _____   10. you are _____

5. they are _____   11. it is _____

6. we will _____   12. he is _____

Directions: Read each sentence. Write the correct contraction on the line.

we're   let's   you're   I'll   we'll   that's

1. _____ the oldest building in the town.

2. Dad said _____ be going on vacation soon.

3. Joe says that _____ moving in two weeks.

4. I think _____ make pizza for dinner.

14   *Reading: Grade 3*

Letter Ladders

Singular means one, and **plural** means more than one. Add **s** to most nouns to make them plural. Add **es** if the singular noun ends in **s, x, z, ch,** or **sh**.

Directions: Write the plural form of each noun on the correct ladder.

banana
whale
patch
orange
wish
class
tiger
flash
scratch
flower
kiss
coin
dish
switch
snake
bus
hoop
tax
key
trail

Add s

Add es

15   *Reading: Grade 3*

Name_____

Plural Endings

Remember, singular means one, and plural means more than one. When a singular noun ends in a consonant and **y**, change the **y** to **i** and add **es**.

Example: cand**y**   cand**ies**

Some singular nouns form plurals with special spellings. You need to memorize them.

Examples: man — men
woman — women
child — children
foot — feet
tooth — teeth
mouse — mice

Directions: Write the plural form of each noun on the candies.

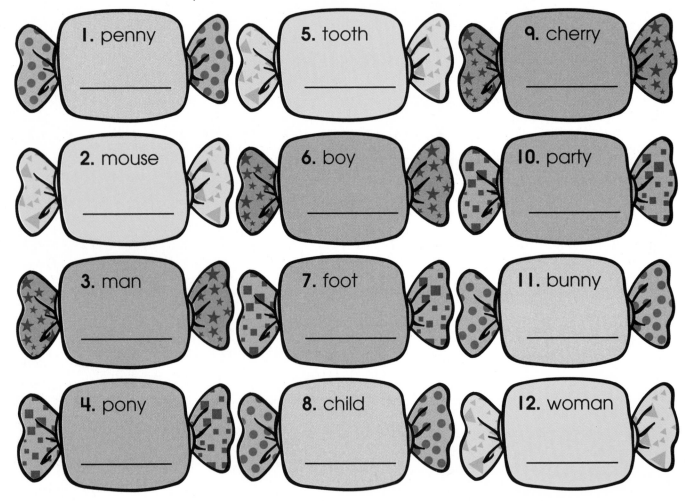

1. penny _____
2. mouse _____
3. man _____
4. pony _____
5. tooth _____
6. boy _____
7. foot _____
8. child _____
9. cherry _____
10. party _____
11. bunny _____
12. woman _____

Building Words

One way to build a new word is to add a prefix to the beginning of a word.
A **prefix** is a word part added to the beginning of a word that changes the
meaning of the word.

Examples:

prefix	+	word	=	new word	Prefix Meaning
re	+	place	=	replace	(again)
un	+	even	=	uneven	(not)
mid	+	air	=	midair	(middle)
in	+	accurate	=	inaccurate	(not)

Directions: Write a new word for each meaning using a prefix from above.

1. paint again   _____
2. not fair   _____
3. not complete   _____
4. the middle of the day   _____
5. not touched   _____
6. write again   _____
7. not clear   _____
8. do again   _____
9. not direct   _____
10. not fit   _____
11. wrap again   _____
12. the middle of summer   _____
13. not true   _____
14. read again   _____
15. the middle of a stream   _____
16. not expensive   _____

Suffixes

Another way to build a new word is to add a suffix to the end of the word. A **suffix** is a word part that is added to the end of a word to change its meaning

Examples:	word	+	suffix	=	new word	(suffix meaning)
	sing	+	er	=	singer	(a person or thing)
	care	+	less	=	careless	(without)
	skill	+	ful	=	skillful	(full of)

er	less	ful

Directions: Write a new word for each meaning using the underlined word and a suffix from above.

1. one who can <u>jump</u>   **jumper**

2. without <u>hope</u> _____

3. full of <u>grace</u> _____

4. without <u>worth</u> _____

5. one who can <u>clean</u> _____

6. full of <u>success</u> _____

7. without <u>use</u> _____

8. one who can <u>read</u> _____

9. without <u>help</u> _____

10. one who can <u>teach</u> _____

11. full of <u>cheer</u> _____

12. full of <u>wonder</u> _____

13. without <u>color</u> _____

14. one who can <u>farm</u> _____

Name_____

Base Words

A word without any prefixes or suffixes is called a **base word** or **root word**. Prefixes and suffixes change a base word's meaning.

Example: The base word in de**frost**ed is **frost**. The prefix is **de** and the suffix is **ed**

Directions: Write the prefix and suffix that was added to each base word.

Prefix	Word	Suffix
1. _____	reconsidered	_____
2. _____	invaluable	_____
3. _____	unstoppable	_____
4. _____	disinterested	_____
5. _____	recoverable	_____
6. _____	inconsiderately	_____
7. _____	misinformed	_____
8. _____	unchanging	_____
9. _____	unlikely	_____
10. _____	distrustful	_____

The Root of the Problem

Directions: Underline the root of each word in the list. Then, circle the root words in the word search. Words may go up, down, across, backwards, and diagonally.

1. planting
2. mending
3. fishing
4. golden
5. swimming
6. certainly
7. suddenly
8. arrows
9. foolish
10. sounds
11. sighing
12. rushing
13. safely
14. asleep
15. longer
16. arms
17. stones
18. bandits

A	P	L	A	N	T	H	S	I	F
R	O	C	E	R	T	A	I	N	O
M	E	N	D	D	N	U	O	S	O
I	A	E	L	P	R	E	K	I	L
W	R	D	O	G	N	O	L	G	E
S	R	D	G	O	R	U	S	H	F
N	O	U	T	S	L	E	E	P	A
V	W	S	T	I	D	N	A	B	S

Syllables

A **syllable** is a smaller part of a word that has a vowel sound. The number of syllables is the number of vowel sounds you hear.

Examples: mouse — **1** syllable
afraid — **2** syllables
stepmother — **3** syllables

To help you say a longer word, you can divide it into syllables . . .

between two consonants — **hap/py**

after a long vowel — **o/pen**

after the consonant when the vowel is short — **cab/in**

to separate prefixes and suffixes — **mis/treat/ment**

Directions: Write the number of syllables you hear in each word.

1. _____ affect

2. _____ feast

3. _____ remember

4. _____ retelling

5. _____ misinformation

6. _____ unorganized

7. _____ threat

8. _____ opposite

9. _____ character

10. _____ unwisely

Directions: Write the word, placing a hyphen between each syllable. You can use a dictionary to help you.

1. ornament _____

2. breakfast _____

3. baby _____

4. repeated _____

5. surprise _____

 Reading: Grade 3

Quilting Bee

Directions: Follow the code to color the quilt squares.

1-syllable words = blue	3-syllable words = green
2-syllable words = red	4-syllable words = yellow

The quilt squares contain the following words:

collecting, eggs, creations, reins, ruffled

Ruth, authority, searched, frolic, plain

constantly, pleasured, unusual, amidst, daughters

drive, hooves, special, interrupted, gossiped

community, directed, peered, instructed, buggy

22 *Reading: Grade 3*

Circle a Synonym

Words that mean the same thing, or almost the same thing, are called **synonyms**.

Directions: Circle a synonym for the **boldfaced** word in each line. Then, select another synonym from the word list to write in the blanks.

Word List		
silky	lively	prickly
slender	sturdy	fatigued

1. **sharp:**   pointed   spear   _____

2. **strong:**   gym   tough   _____

3. **smooth:**   velvety   chocolate   _____

4. **narrow:**   bridge   thin   _____

5. **frisky:**   playful   haughty   _____

6. **exhausted:**   naughty   tired   _____

Synonym Snob!

Sydney is a synonym snob! She hates to use the same words as everybody else. Help Sydney say her student council speech using super synonyms! Change each underlined word to a more exciting synonym. You may use the word list below for ideas.

Word List

brainy	balmy	incredibly	bright
good	luminous	outrageously	kind
morning	superb	hello	polite
attend	fantastic	clever	elect
humid	hot	intelligent	orderly
pleasant	extremely	prepared	wonderful

   Hi, my name is Sydney. I go to Aloha School in warm and sunny Hawaii. I would like to be on student council because I can do a great job. I am very smart, and I work hard. Also, I am very organized and nice to people. Those are the reasons you should vote for me!

Directions: Write Sydney's new speech on the lines below:

_____

_____

_____

_____

Antonyms Are Opposites

Words with opposite meanings are called **antonyms**.
Directions: Circle the pair of antonyms in each box. Complete each sentence with one of the circled words.

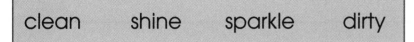

| clean | shine | sparkle | dirty |

Taking out the garbage made my hands _____.

After I take a bath, I feel very _____.

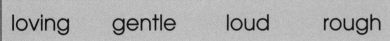

| loving | gentle | loud | rough |

My new cat was very _____ with her kittens.

The monkeys are _____ with each other when they play.

| polite | chatty | horrible | rude |

Shouting out in class is very _____.

The student was very _____ to her teacher.

| tall | mean | kind | kite |

The _____ boy had no friends.

A _____ friend is a nice friend to have.

Antonyms Puzzle

Directions: Fill in the crossword puzzle below. Use the clues in the word list, except choose each word's **opposite** meaning. Good luck!

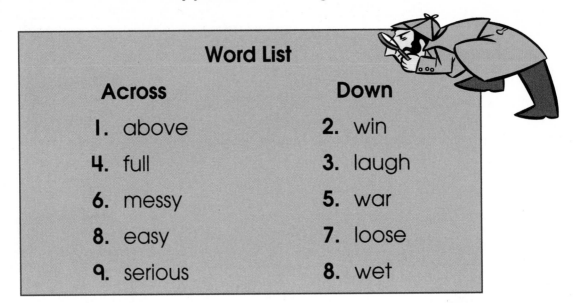

Word List

Across	Down
1. above	2. win
4. full	3. laugh
6. messy	5. war
8. easy	7. loose
9. serious	8. wet

Name _____

Homophones

Words that are pronounced the same, but have different spellings and different meanings, are called **homophones**.

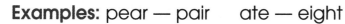

Examples: pear — pair   ate — eight

Directions: Write the correct homophone to complete each sentence.

1. (red / read)

   I _____ the book.

   My book is _____ .

2. (pear / pair / pare)

   I ate the delicious _____ .

   I have a _____ of gloves.

   Will you _____ the fruit?

3. (sun / son)

   They have a polite _____ .

   The _____ is shining today.

4. (ate / eight)

   I _____ pizza for lunch.

   I bought _____ pens.

5. (way / weigh)

   How much do you _____ ?

   Do you know the _____ there?

6. (to / two / too)

   We have _____ apples.

   We went _____ the store.

   I have an apple, _____ .

7. (one / won)

   I _____ the race.

   I have _____ brother.

8. (I / eye)

   Dust blew into my _____ .

   _____ blinked to get rid of it.

Directions: Circle the homophone that names the picture.

1. not/knot   2. hour/our   3. board/bored   4. due/dew

Name _____

Be a Busy Bee

Directions: Underline the correct homophone for each sentence.

1. In medieval days, (nights, knights) wore armor.

2. The (be, bee) was busy buzzing around his head.

3. Some people like nuts on their ice cream, but I prefer mine (plain, plane)

4. Our teacher read us the tall (tail, tale) of Paul Bunyan.

5. We had to find a partner and run the relay as a (pear, pair).

6. On a hot summer day, it's fun to play at the (beach, beech).

7. Is it (to, too, two) late?

8. If Rebecca wins the game, she can (chews, choose) a prize.

9. A baby (deer, dear) is called a fawn.

10. Does anyone (no, know) the correct answer?

11. Kayla and Tarisha (write, right) letters to each other.

12. It is fun to get a letter in the (male, mail).

13. Mrs. Jackson (wears, wares) a curly wig.

14. Little black (aunts, ants) invaded the family picnic.

15. We also had to (shoo, shoe) away many flies.

16. Mike and Kyle (through, threw) a baseball back and forth.

17. King George II (reigned, rained) in England.

18. Let's (wade, weighed) in the water.

Nouns

Nouns are words that tell the names of people, places, or things.

Directions: Read the words below. Then, write them in the correct column.

goat	Mrs. Jackson	girl
beach	tree	song
mouth	park	Jean Rivers
finger	flower	New York
Kevin Jones	Elm City	Frank Gates
Main Street	theater	skates
River Park	father	boy

Person

Place

Thing

_____   _____   _____

_____   _____   _____

_____   _____   _____

_____   _____   _____

_____   _____   _____

_____   _____   _____

_____   _____   _____

Common Nouns

Common nouns are nouns that name any member of a group of people, places, or things, rather than specific people, places, or things.

Directions: Read the sentences below and write the common noun found in each sentence.

Example: ___socks___ My socks do not match.

1. _____ The bird could not fly.

2. _____ Ben likes to eat jelly beans.

3. _____ I am going to meet my mother.

4. _____ We will go swimming in the lake tomorrow.

5. _____ I hope the flowers will grow quickly.

6. _____ We colored eggs together.

7. _____ It is easy to ride a bicycle.

8. _____ My cousin is very tall.

9. _____ Ted and Jane went fishing in their boat.

10. _____ They won a prize yesterday.

11. _____ She fell down and twisted her ankle.

12. _____ My brother was born today.

13. _____ She went down the slide.

14. _____ Ray went to the doctor today.

Proper Nouns

Proper nouns are names of specific people, places, or things. Proper nouns begin with a capital letter.

Directions: Read the sentences below and circle the proper nouns found in each sentence.

Example: (Aunt Frances) gave me a puppy for my birthday.

1. We lived on Jackson Street before we moved to our new house.

2. Angela's birthday party is tomorrow night.

3. We drove through Cheyenne, Wyoming, on our way home.

4. Dr. Charles always gives me a treat for not crying.

5. George Washington was our first president.

6. Our class took a field trip to the Johnson Flower Farm.

7. Uncle Jack lives in New York City.

8. Amy and Elizabeth are best friends.

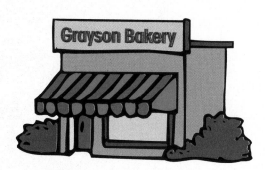

9. We buy doughnuts at the Grayson Bakery.

10. My favorite movie is *E.T.*

11. We flew to Miami, Florida, in a plane.

12. We go to Riverfront Stadium to watch the baseball games.

13. Mr. Fields is a wonderful music teacher.

14. My best friend is Tom Dunlap.

Name _____

Little Words Mean a Lot

A **pronoun** is a word that takes the place of a noun.

Directions: Above each **bold** word below, write a pronoun that could replace it.

she	it	her	we	he	his	I	him	they	your

1. Uncle Nick shouted at Mus Mus as **Uncle Nick** walked to the kitchen.

2. **Lucy** ran to **Lucy's** mother in tears.

3. **The Littles** crowded up to the kitchen door.

4. Granny Little said, "**Granny Little** wouldn't believe it if **Granny Little** didn't see it with these old eyes."

5. Lucy said, "**Mus Mus**" is a cute name.

6. **Will and Tom** have gone to get some leftovers.

7. **Uncle Nick** kept on writing **Uncle Nick's** life story.

8. **Mrs. Little** whispered, "Don't bother **Uncle Nick**."

9. Granny Little turned **Granny Little's** back on **Uncle Nick**.

10. Tom told Uncle Nick, "**Lucy and Tom** want to read **Uncle Nick's** book."

they
your
her

he   she

we

it

Pronouns

Singular Pronouns

I me my mine

you your yours

he she it her

hers his its him

Plural Pronouns

we us our ours

you your yours

they them their theirs

Directions: Underline the pronouns in each sentence.

1. Mom told us to wash our hands.

2. Did you go to the store?

3. We should buy him a present.

4. I called you about their party.

5. Our house had damage on its roof.

6. They want to give you a prize at our party.

7. My cat ate her sandwich.

8. Your coat looks like his coat.

Name _____

Possessive Nouns

Directions: Circle the correct possessive noun for each sentence and write it in the blank.

Example: One ____girl's____ mother is a teacher.
(girl's)   girls'

1. The _____ tail is long.
cat's   cats'

2. One _____ baseball bat is aluminum.
boy's   boys'

3. The _____ aprons are white.
waitresses'   waitress's

4. My _____ apple pie is the best!
grandmother's   grandmothers'

5. My five _____ uniforms are dirty.
brother's   brothers'

6. The _____ doll is pretty.
child's   childs'

7. These _____ collars are different colors.
dog's   dogs'

8. The _____ tail is short.
cow's   cows'

Possessive Pronouns

Possessive pronouns show ownership.

Example: his hat, **her** shoes, **our** dog

We can use these pronouns before a noun:
my, our, you, his, her, its, their

Example: That is **my** bike.

We can use these pronouns on their own:
mine, yours, ours, his, hers, theirs, its

Example: That is **mine**.

Directions: Write each sentence again, using a pronoun instead of the words in bold letters. Be sure to use capitals and periods.

Example:

My **dog's** bowl is brown.   **Its** bowl is brown.

1. That is **Lisa's** book. _____

2. This is **my pencil**. _____

3. This hat is **your hat**. _____

4. Fifi is **Kevin's** cat. _____

5. That beautiful house is **our home**.

_____

6. **The gerbil's** cage is too small.

_____

Articles "A" and "An"

An **article** is a word that points out a singular noun in a sentence.

Use the article **a** before words beginning with consonants.

Examples: I saw **a b**ird fly into a tree.
The bird was building **a n**est.

Use the article **an** before words beginning with vowels or vowel sounds.

Examples: An eagle perched on a branch.
There was **an e**gg in its nest.

Directions: Write the correct article, **a** or **an**, on the line.

1. I have _an_ aunt named Mary.

2. We went to _____ movie last night.

3. Mark wrote _____ long letter.

4. We took _____ English test.

5. Ned has _____ old bicycle.

6. We had _____ ice-cream cone.

7. Maggie ate _____ orange for breakfast.

8. They saw _____ deer on their trip.

9. Steve thought the car was _____ ugly color.

10. Emily bought _____ new pair of skates.

11. He was _____ officer in the army.

12. _____ elephant is such a large animal.

13. Arizona is _____ state in the Southwest.

14. Rosa was _____ infielder on her softball team.

15. Jordan ate _____ apricot for a snack.

Verbs

A **verb** is a word that can show action. A verb can also tell what someone or something is or is like.

Examples: The boats **sail** on Lake Michigan.
We **eat** dinner at 6:00.
I **am** ten years old.
The clowns **were** funny.

Directions: Circle the verb in each sentence.

1. John sips milk.

2. They throw the football.

3. We hiked in the woods.

4. I enjoy music.

5. My friend smiles often.

6. A lion hunts for food.

7. We ate lunch at noon.

8. Fish swim in the ocean.

9. My team won the game.

10. They were last in line.

11. The wind howled during the night.

12. Kangaroos live in Australia.

13. The plane flew into the clouds.

14. We recorded the song.

15. They forgot the directions.

37 *Reading: Grade 3*

Verbs

When a verb tells what one person or thing is doing now, it usually ends in **s**.
Example: She **sings**.

When a verb is used with **you**, **I**, or **we**,
we do not add an **s**.

Example: I **sing**.

Directions: Write the correct verb in
each sentence.

Example:

I _____write_____ a newspaper about our street.   **writes, write**

I. My sister _____ me sometimes.   **helps, help**

2. She _____ the pictures.   **draw, draws**

3. We _____ them together.   **delivers, deliver**

4. I _____ the news about all the people.   **tell, tells**

5. Mr. Macon _____ the most beautiful flowers.   **grow, grows**

6. Mrs. Jones _____ to her plants.   **talks, talk**

7. Kevin Turner _____ his dog loose everyday.   **lets, let**

8. Little Mikey Smith _____ lost once a week.   **get, gets**

9. You may _____ I live on an interesting street.   **thinks, think**

10. We _____ it's the best street in town.   **say, says**

Irregular Verbs

Past-tense verbs that are not formed
by adding **ed** are called **irregular verbs**.

Example:

Present	**Past**
sing	sang

Directions: Circle the present-tense verb in each pair of irregular verbs.

I. won win		**4.** tell told		**7.** say said	
2. feel felt		**5.** eat ate		**8.** came come	
3. built build		**6.** blew blow		**9.** grew grow	

Directions: Write the past tense of each irregular verb.

I. throw _____   4. sing _____   7. swim _____

2. wear _____   5. lose _____   8. sit _____

3. hold _____   6. fly _____   9. sell _____

Directions: In each blank, write the past tense of the irregular verb in
parentheses.

I. I _____ my library book to my sister. (give)

2. She _____ for school before I did. (leave)

3. She _____ the bus at the corner. (catch)

4. My sister _____ my book on the way to school. (lose)

5. My sister _____ back to find it. (go)

Irregular Verbs

The verb **be** is different from all other verbs. The present-tense forms of **be** are **am**, **is**, and **are**. The past-tense forms of **be** are **was** and **were**. The verb **to be** is written in the following ways:

singular: I am, you are, he is, she is, it is
plural: we are, you are, they are

Directions: Choose the correct form of **be** from the words in the box and write it in each sentence. Some sentences may have more than one correct form of **be**.

| are | am | is | was | were |

Example:

I _____ **am** _____ feeling good at this moment.

1. My sister _____ a good singer.

2. You _____ going to the store with me.

3. Sandy _____ at the movies last week.

4. Rick and Tom _____ best friends.

5. He _____ happy about the surprise.

6. The cat _____ hungry.

7. I _____ going to the ball game.

8. They _____ silly.

9. I _____ glad to help my mother.

 Reading: Grade 3

Helping Verbs

A **helping verb** is a word used with an action verb.

Examples: **might**, **shall**, and **are**

Directions: Write a helping verb from the box with each action verb.

can	could	must	might
may	would	should	will
shall	did	does	do
had	have	has	am
are	were	is	
be	being	been	

Example:

Tomorrow, I _____might_____ play soccer.

1. Mom _____ buy my new soccer shoes tonight.

2. Yesterday, my old soccer shoes _____ ripped by the cat.

3. I _____ going to ask my brother to go to the game.

4. He usually _____ not like soccer.

5. But, he _____ go with me because I am his sister.

6. He _____ promised to watch the entire soccer game.

7. He has _____ helping me with my homework.

8. I _____ spell a lot better because of his help.

9. Maybe I _____ finish the semester at the top of my class.

Name _____

Linking Verbs

A **linking verb** does not show action. Instead, it links the subject of the sentence with a noun or adjective in the predicate. **Am, is, are, was**, and **were** are linking verbs.

Example:
Thomas Jefferson **was** President of the United States.

Directions: Write a linking verb in each blank.

1. The class's writing assignment _____ a report on U.S. Presidents.

2. The reports _____ due tomorrow.

3. I _____ glad I chose to write about Thomas Jefferson, the third president of our country.

4. Early in his life, he _____ the youngest delegate to the First Continental Congress.

5. The colonies _____ angry at England.

6. Thomas Jefferson _____ a great writer, so he was asked to help write the Declaration of Independence.

7. The signing of that document _____ a historical event.

8. Later, as president, Jefferson _____ responsible for the Louisiana Purchase.

9. He _____ the first president to live in the White House.

10. Americans _____ fortunate today for the part Thomas Jefferson played in our country's history.

Review

Verb tenses can be in the past, present, or future.

Directions: Match each sentence with the correct verb tense.
(**Think:** When did each thing happen?)

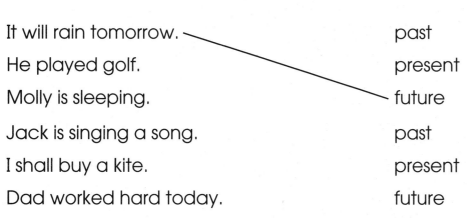

It will rain tomorrow.	past
He played golf.	present
Molly is sleeping.	future
Jack is singing a song.	past
I shall buy a kite.	present
Dad worked hard today.	future

Past

Present

Future

Directions: Change the verb to the tense shown.

1. Jenny played with her new friend. (present)

_____

2. Bobby is talking to him. (future)

_____

3. Holly and Angie walk here. (past)

_____

Marvelous Modifiers

Words that describe are called **adjectives**.
Directions: Circle the adjectives in the sentences below.

1. Lucas stared at the cool white paint in the can.

2. The green grass was marked with bits of white paint.

3. The naughty twins needed a warm soapy bath.

4. The painters worked with large rollers.

5. Lucas thought it was a great joke.

Directions: For each noun below, write two descriptive adjectives. Then, write a sentence using all three words.

1. marshmallows   _____   _____

_____

_____

2. airplane   _____   _____

_____

_____

3. beach   _____   _____

_____

_____

4. summer   _____   _____

_____

_____

Adverbs

An **adverb** is a word that can describe a verb. It tells how, when, or where an action takes place.

Example:
The snow fell **quietly**. (how)
It snowed **yesterday**. (when)
It fell **everywhere**. (where)

Directions: Circle the adverbs in the story. Then, write them under the correct category in the chart.

The snow began early in the day. Huge snowflakes floated gracefully to the ground. Soon, the ground was covered with a blanket of white. Later, the wind began to blow briskly. Outside, the snow drifted into huge mounds. When the snow stopped, the children went outdoors. Then, they played in the snow there. They went sledding nearby. Others happily built snow forts. Joyfully, the boys and girls ran around. They certainly enjoyed the snow.

How	When	Where

45

Adjectives and Adverbs

An **adjective** is used to describe a noun. An **adverb** describes a verb or an action.

Example:
We went into the **busy** pet store. (adjective)
Dad and I walked **quickly** through the mall. (adverb)

Directions: Write an adjective or an adverb to describe each **bold** word.

Adjectives		Adverbs	
white	many	immediately	straight
adorable	best	excitedly	pitifully

1. Dad and I **went** _____ to the back wall.

2. We saw _____ animal **cages**.

3. The _____ **puppies** interested me most.

4. One little beagle **wiggled** _____.

5. I _____ **knew** this was the one I wanted.

6. He was black and brown with _____ **spots**.

7. He **whined** _____.

8. A puppy would be the _____ **present** I could have.

Commas

Commas are used to separate words in a series of three or more.

Example: My favorite fruits are apples, bananas, and oranges.

Directions: Put commas where they are needed in each sentence.

1. Please buy milk eggs bread and cheese.

2. I need a folder paper and pencils for school.

3. Some good pets are cats dogs gerbils fish and rabbits.

4. Aaron Mike and Matt went to the baseball game.

5. Major forms of transportation are planes trains and automobiles.

47 *Reading: Grade 3*

Articles and Commas

Directions: Write **a** or **an** in each blank. Put commas where they are needed in the paragraphs below.

Owls

_____ owl is _____ bird of prey. This means it hunts small animals. Owls catch insects fish and birds. Mice are _____ owl's favorite dinner. Owls like protected places, such as trees burrows or barns. Owls make noises that sound like hoots screeches or even barks. _____ owl's feathers may be black brown gray or white.

A Zoo for You

_____ zoo is _____ excellent place for keeping animals. Zoos have mammals birds reptiles and amphibians. Some zoos have domestic animals, such as rabbits sheep and goats. Another name for this type of zoo is _____ petting zoo. In some zoos, elephants lions and tigers live in open country. This is because _____ enormous animal needs open space for roaming.

48 *Reading: Grade 3*

Subjects and Predicates

Every sentence has two parts. The **subject** tells who or what the sentence is about. The **predicate** tells what the subject does, did, is, or has.

Example: The snowman is melting.

subject   predicate

Directions: Draw one line under the subject and two lines under the predicate.

1. The horses are racing to the finish line.

2. Mrs. Porter went to see Jack's teacher.

3. Josh moved to Atlanta, Georgia.

4. Monica's birthday is July 15th.

5. The ball rolled into the street.

6. Tammy planned a surprise party.

7. The winning team received a trophy.

8. The fireworks displays were fantastic.

9. The heavy rain drove everyone inside.

10. Adam looked everywhere for his book.

11. You can hear the band outside.

12. My family has tickets for the football game.

13. Cats are furry and soft.

14. The police officer stopped the traffic.

15. All of the team played in the soccer tournament.

Making Sentences

Remember, a sentence must tell a complete thought.

Directions: Draw a line from each beginning to an ending that makes a complete sentence.

1. John and Patty attend

2. The band camp lasts

3. All the kids bring

4. John plays the clarinet,

5. Each day the kids

6. The teacher helps them

7. On the last day,

for two fun-filled weeks.

and Patty plays the flute.

practice music together.

a band camp every summer.

they give a final concert.

improve their performance.

their own instruments.

Sentence Building

A **sentence** can tell more and more.

Directions: Read the sentence parts. Write a word on each line to make each sentence tell more.

1. Mrs. _____ bought a sweater.
      Who?

2. Mrs. _____ bought a sweater and two _____.
      Who?   What?

3. Mrs. _____ bought a sweater and two _____
      Who?   What?

   before leaving the _____ .
                        Where?

4. Mrs. _____ bought a sweater and two _____
      Who?   What?

   before leaving the _____ to pick up _____.
                        Where?   Who?

5. Mrs. _____ bought a sweater and two _____
      Who?   What?

   before leaving the _____ to pick up_____
                        Where?   Who?

   at _____ .
       When?

Paragraph Form

A **paragraph** is a group of sentences about one main idea. When writing a paragraph, remember these rules:

1. **Indent** the first line.
2. **Capitalize** the first word of each sentence.
3. **Punctuate** each sentence.

Directions: Rewrite each paragraph correctly by following the three rules.

the number of teeth you have depends on your age a baby has no teeth at all gradually, milk teeth, or baby teeth, begin to grow later, these teeth fall out and permanent teeth appear by the age of twenty-five, you should have thirty-two permanent teeth.

_____

_____

_____

_____

my family is going to Disneyland tomorrow we plan to arrive early my dad will take my little sister to Fantasyland first meanwhile, my brother and I will visit Frontierland and Adventureland after lunch, we will all meet to go to Tomorrowland

_____

_____

_____

_____

Name _____

Topic Sentences

Remember, a paragraph is a group of sentences that tells about one main idea. One of the sentences states the main idea. That sentence is called the **topic sentence**. The topic sentence is often the first sentence in the paragraph

Example:

<u>Three planets in our solar system have rings around them.</u> The planets with rings are Saturn, Uranus, and Jupiter. The rings are actually thin belts of rocks that orbit the planets. Saturn is the most famous ringed planet.

Directions: Underline the topic sentence in the paragraph below.

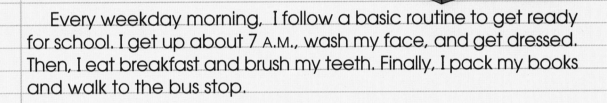

Every weekday morning, I follow a basic routine to get ready for school. I get up about 7 A.M., wash my face, and get dressed. Then, I eat breakfast and brush my teeth. Finally, I pack my books and walk to the bus stop.

Directions: Write a topic sentence for a paragraph about each idea.

1. Homework: _____

_____

2. Breakfast: _____

_____

3. Neighbors: _____

_____

4. Friends: _____

_____

5. Camping: _____

_____

Support Sentences

Remember, the topic sentence gives the main idea of a paragraph. The **support sentences** give details about the main idea. Each support sentence must relate to the main idea.

Directions: Underline the topic sentence in the paragraph. Cross out the sentence that is not a support sentence. Write another to replace it.

Throwing a surprise birthday party can be exciting but tricky. The honored person must not hear a word about the party! On the day of the party, everyone should arrive early. A snack may ruin your appetite. _____

_____

Directions: Write two support sentences to go with each topic sentence.

1. Giving a dog a bath can be a real challenge!

    A. _____

    B. _____

2. I can still remember how much fun we had that day!

    A. _____

    B. _____

3. Sometimes I like to imagine what our prehistoric world was like.

    A. _____

    B. _____

4. A daily newspaper features many kinds of news.

    A. _____

    B. _____

Paragraph Plan

Here is an example of a plan you can follow when writing a paragraph.

Paragraph Plan	Example
Step 1: Choose a topic	Step 1: Helping with household chores
Step 2: Brainstorm for ideas.	Step 2: Cleaning room Taking out trash Washing dishes Feeding pets
Step 3: Write a topic sentence.	Step 3: Most kids help their families with household chores.
Step 4: Use ideas from Step 2 to write support sentences.	Step 4: Some kids take out the trash every day. Many kids like to feed their pets or help with the dishes. Almost every kid has to keep a neat room.
Step 5: Write the topic and support sentences together in a paragraph.	Step 5: Most kids help their families with household chores. Some kids take out the trash every day. Many kids like to feed their pets or help with the dishes. Almost every kid has to keep a neat room.

Directions: Use the paragraph plan to write a paragraph on the next page. Choose a topic from the group below.

A Day to Remember

Being a Good Friend

Staying Healthy

Paragraph Plan

Directions: Follow the paragraph plan described on the previous page.

A Day to Remember   Being a Good Friend   Staying Healthy

Step 1: Topic _____   _____

Step 2: Ideas _____   _____

_____   _____

_____   _____

Step 3: Topic Sentence _____

_____

Step 4: Support Sentences _____

_____

_____

_____

_____

Step 5: Write Paragraph

_____

_____

_____

_____

_____

_____

_____

Step-by-Step Car Wash

"Hey, Tim! Will you help me wash the car today?" asked my dad.

"Sure, Dad," I answered.

"Great, let's get organized!"

Directions: Below are the steps you need to follow to wash a car, but they are all mixed up. Number the steps in order. Mark an **X** in front of any steps that are not needed.

_____ Let the car dry in the sun.

_____ Bring the hose over to the car.

_____ Pick a sunny day (not a rainy day)!

_____ Eat a hamburger.

_____ Move the car out of the garage into the driveway.

_____ Fill the bucket with soap and water.

_____ Brush your hair.

_____ Rinse the car again.

_____ Dance around the car.

_____ Wash down the car with water for the first rinse.

_____ Take a big sponge, dip it into the soapy water, and make slow circles with the sponge to clean the car.

State Search

Following directions means reading and doing exactly what the words say to do.

Directions: Follow the directions below the list of places. Then, put a check in the box after you complete each direction.

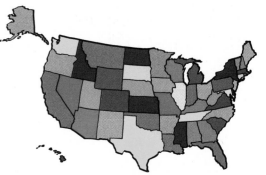

California	Ohio	Utah	Arizona
North Dakota	Mississippi	Oklahoma	Texas
Georgia	Florida	Wyoming	Maine
Vermont	Alaska	South Carolina	

☐   **1.** Draw a red ring around the name of the state that has only one syllable.

☐   **2.** Draw a blue box around the name of any state with two words in its name.

☐   **3.** Draw a green line under the name of each state that does not end in a vowel.

☐   **4.** Draw a yellow box around the name of each state that has a one-word name with four syllables.

☐   **5.** Draw a purple check by the name of each state that ends with a vowel other than **a** or **e**.

☐   **6.** Write the names of three states that you have not used in alphabetical order.

_____   _____   _____

Main Message

The **main idea** is the most important idea about a topic, or the message a writer wants you to understand.

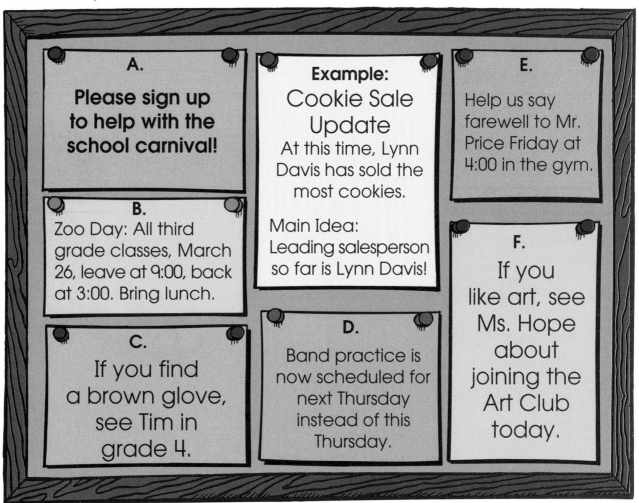

Directions: Write the letter of the note that matches each main idea.

◯ **1.** Band practice has been postponed for a week.

◯ **2.** Students are encouraged to take part in the school carnival.

◯ **3.** Tim lost one of his brown gloves.

◯ **4.** Everyone at school is invited to the going-away party for Mr. Price.

◯ **5.** On March 26, the third graders will spend the day at the zoo.

◯ **6.** Ms. Hope is looking for new members for the Art Club.

Name _____

Get the Point

The main idea can be the point or purpose of the entire story. Also, each paragraph within a story may have its own main idea.

Directions: Read the story. Then, write an **X** next to each correct main idea.

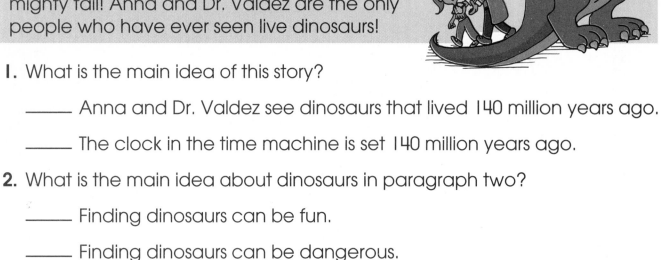

Anna and Dr. Valdez open their eyes and step outside of the time machine. They have landed in the middle of a jungle. Dr. Valdez checks the time clock. It is set at 140 million years ago!

Suddenly, they hear crashing thunder. Anna and Dr. Valdez turn around and see a giant Apatosaurus and a Tyrannosaurus Rex. The two dinosaurs can't see Anna and Dr. Valdez, but a very unfriendly looking Stegosaurus does.

Anna and Dr. Valdez jump back into their machine. They quickly set the time for the present. Snap! Crackle! Pop! The machine leaves for the present just as the Stegosaurus swings its mighty tail! Anna and Dr. Valdez are the only people who have ever seen live dinosaurs!

1. What is the main idea of this story?

    _____ Anna and Dr. Valdez see dinosaurs that lived 140 million years ago.

    _____ The clock in the time machine is set 140 million years ago.

2. What is the main idea about dinosaurs in paragraph two?

    _____ Finding dinosaurs can be fun.

    _____ Finding dinosaurs can be dangerous.

3. What is the main reason Anna and Dr. Valdez jump back into their machine'

    _____ They have seen enough dinosaurs.

    _____ The Stegosaurus looks unfriendly.

4. What is a good title for this story?

    _____ A Close Call   _____ Time Travel

All About Gators

Directions: Read the paragraphs and write the answer to each question in a complete sentence.

Alligators are reptiles. They are related to crocodiles, but they have wider snouts than crocodiles do. Also, unlike crocodiles, all of the alligators' teeth are hidden from view when their mouths are closed.

American alligators live in or near swamps, lakes, and streams of the southeastern states. They eat fish, frogs, birds, turtles, and small mammals. Occasionally, alligators will even eat larger mammals such as dogs or pigs.

After the female mates in the spring, she prepares a special nest constructed of mud and water plants. She lays from 30 to 80 eggs in the nest. The sun warms the eggs, and they hatch in about 60 days. When the eggs hatch, the young call for their mother. The mother carries the babies to a nearby pond. They stay there for the first year under their mother's protection.

1. What do newly hatched alligators do first?_____

_____

2. About how long does it take for an alligator egg to hatch?_____

_____

3. What do alligators eat?_____

_____

4. What kind of an animal is an alligator?_____

5. Which animal is the alligator related to? _____

_____

6. How are alligators different from crocodiles? _____

_____

Worth More Than Words

A **conclusion** is a decision you make after thinking about information you have been given. Often, you can judge details in a picture to help you form a conclusion.

Directions: Write an **X** in the box next to each conclusion that makes sense.

1. ☐ It is a very hot day.

2. ☐ The beach is a popular place to go.

3. ☐ The beach is a quiet place to study.

4. ☐ Some people picnic at the beach.

5. ☐ A lifeguard helps protect swimmers.

6. ☐ It is hard to nap at a noisy beach.

7. ☐ Sailing is just for kids.

8. ☐ Sailing and swimming are fun water sports.

9. ☐ Every town has a beach.

10. ☐ A person drowned at the beach.

Directions: Write a sentence telling your own conclusion about the beach.

_____

_____

_____

62 *Reading: Grade 3*

Name _____

Judging a Book by Its Cover

When you use **critical thinking**, often you are using the information you have and your experiences to make a judgment.

Directions: Read the book titles. Write two facts or kinds of information you would expect to find in each book.

1. _____   _____

2. _____   _____

3. _____   _____

4. _____   _____

5. _____   _____

6. _____   _____

7. _____   _____

8. _____   _____

9. _____   _____

10. _____   _____

11. _____   _____

If . . . Then

Directions: Underline the **cause** with red and the **effect** with blue.

1. Dorothy lay down to take a nap, for the long walk had made her tired.

2. The ladder they had made was so heavy, they couldn't pull it over the wall.

3. The group realized they should be careful in this dainty country because the people could be hurt easily.

4. The Joker had many cracks over his body because he always tried to stand on his head.

5. The china princess had stiff joints on the store shelf, because she had traveled so far from her country.

6. The Lion attacked the great spider, because it had been eating the animals of the forest.

7. The forest animals bowed to the Lion as their king, because he had killed their enemy.

8. The animals asked the Lion to save them, because he was thought of as King of the Beasts.

9. Traveling through the forest was difficult, because the forest floor was covered with thick grass and muddy holes.

10. Dorothy loved the china princess and wanted to take her home, because she was beautiful.

What's Next?

Directions: Write two sentences that predict different possible outcomes.

The smoke from the oven rose in the air toward the smoke detector.

1. _____

2. _____

The crowd cheered wildly as the football player ran toward the goal line.

1. _____

2. _____

Bob and Kelly were on their way to the movie when Kelly realized she had left her money at home.

1. _____

2. _____

When Rob arrived for the museum tour, he found that the tour had started ten minutes earlier.

1. _____

2. _____

Just as Sam was to go on stage for the class play, he realized he had forgotten his lines.

1. _____

2. _____

Extra! Extra! Read All About It!

Newspaper reporters have very important jobs. They have to catch a reader's attention and, at the same time, tell the facts.

Newspaper reporters write their stories by answering the questions **who**, **what**, **where**, **when**, **why**, and **how**.

Directions: Think about a book you have just read and answer the questions below.

Who: **Who** is the story about?

_____

What: **What** happened to the main character?

_____

Where: **Where** does the story take place?

_____

When: **When** does the story take place?

_____

Why: **Why** do these story events happen?

_____

How: **How** do these events happen?

_____

Extra! Extra! Read All About It! cont.

Directions: Use your answers on the previous page to write a newspaper article about the book you read.

BIG CITY TIMES

_____

(Write a catchy title for your article.)

_____

_____

_____

_____

_____

_____

_____

_____

Write Your Own Story

You may want to create a story just for fun! Once you have chosen the kind of story you want to write, you should brainstorm for ideas. But remember, a good story should have a beginning, a middle, and an end. You can use an outline to organize your ideas.

Directions: Write your ideas for a story to complete this outline.

Kind of Story (mystery, adventure, etc.) _____

   I. Setting (where and when the story takes place)

   A. Where _____ Description _____

   _____

   B. When _____

  II. Characters (people in the story)

   A. Name _____ Description _____

   B. Name _____ Description _____

   C. Name _____ Description _____

   D. Name _____ Description _____

 III. Plot (events of the story) List main events in order.

   A. _____

   _____

   B. _____

   _____

   C. _____

   _____

   D. _____

   _____

Right in Between

Guide words tell you the first and last word that appears on a dictionary page. The **entry word** you are looking for will appear on a page if it comes between the guide words in alphabetical order.

Directions: Underline the words in each group that would be found on a page with the given guide words.

fish / five	**evergreen / eye**	**level / love**	**pickle / plaster**
fight	event	lullaby	pint
fist	edge	leave	polo
first	ewe	look	prize
finish	evil	light	please
file	eagle	loud	planet
frisky	evolve	low	piglet
fit	evaporate	letter	palace

tan / time	**heaven / hundred**	**candle / create**	**zenith / zone**
truck	hairy	coil	zoo
tail	horrible	crater	zinnia
toast	hungry	corner	zodiac
thicket	honest	creep	zest
tepee	hindsight	cavern	zeal
tasty	hunter	candid	zebra
tease	help	cable	zephyr

Between the Goalposts

Directions: Circle each football word that would appear alphabetically between each pair of guide words.

heart – hooray

huddle	halfback
hike	handoff
helmet	holding

penalty – pompom

pass	punt
pads	play
pennant	practice

table – track

tackle	touchdown
team	trap
trophy	tailback

back – blitz

bowl	backfield
band	block
bleacher	ball

score – stadium

safety	sweep
sack	second
screen	snap

camera – college

coach	chalk
center	champion
corner	catch

first – fullback

field	flanker
football	fumble
flag	first

gallop – grill

guard	grass
goal	game
gridiron	gain

Review Consonant Digraphs

Remember, a consonant digraph is two or three letters together that make one sound.

Directions: Write the letter of the word that best completes the sentence.

a. knew	e. thorny	i. chest	m. wrote
b. thermos	f. beneath	j. bush	n. shovel
c. where	g. think	k. wrong	
d. character	h. showed	l. crunch	

1. I __m__ a story about a search for hidden riches.
2. The main __d__ was a man who searched for buried treasure.
3. He walked for miles and drank water from a __b__.
4. The map he used __h__ an oddly shaped rock.
5. He found the rock and reached __f__ it.
6. Somehow, he __a__ that nothing would be there.
7. He thought about __c__ he could look next.
8. He noticed a green __j__ growing nearby.
9. The explorer shoved its __e__ branches aside.
10. Then, he reached for a __n__ and began to dig.
11. After digging for awhile, he heard a loud __l__.
12. The sound made him __g__ he had hit a rock.
13. He was definitely __k__ !
14. It was a __i__ filled with shiny jewels and gold.

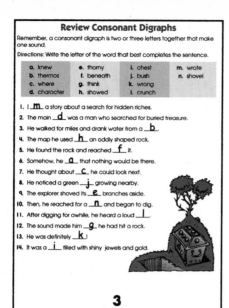

3

Vowel Digraphs

A **vowel digraph** is two vowels together that make one sound. The vowel digraphs **ei** and **ey** can have the sound of long **a** or long **e**.

Examples: **long a sound**
ei in eight
ey in they

long e sound
ei in ceiling
ey in monkey

Directions: Write long **a** or long **e** for the sound of the vowel digraph in each underlined word.

1. The people next door are my <u>neighbors</u>. __long a__
2. <u>They</u> are very friendly. __long a__
3. The son is <u>eighteen</u> years old. __long a__
4. They made us a <u>turkey</u> on Thanksgiving Day. __long e__
5. I learned that a turkey is not a bird of <u>prey</u>. __long a__
6. Once we lost the <u>key</u> to our front door. __long e__
7. We paid <u>money</u> to have the door opened. __long e__
8. The locksmith gave my dad a <u>receipt</u> for it. __long e__
9. That week, Dad also had to fix the <u>ceiling</u>. __long e__
10. He spent a total of <u>eighty</u> dollars. __long a__
11. Dad earns money by loading <u>freight</u> at work. __long a__
12. A shipment of <u>sleighs</u> came in last week. __long a__
13. Dad had to <u>survey</u> the large boxes. __long a__
14. The <u>weight</u> of the shipment was very heavy. __long a__

4

The Tie Thief

The vowel digraph **ie** can have the sound of long **i** or long **e**.

Examples: **long i sound**
ie in tie

long e sound
ie in thief

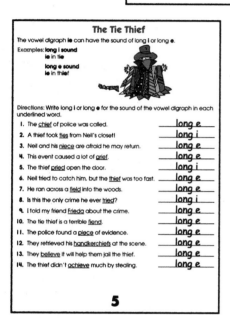

Directions: Write long **i** or long **e** for the sound of the vowel digraph in each underlined word.

1. The <u>chief</u> of police was called. __long e__
2. A thief took <u>ties</u> from Neil's closet! __long i__
3. Neil and his <u>niece</u> are afraid he may return. __long e__
4. This event caused a lot of <u>grief</u>. __long e__
5. The thief <u>pried</u> open the door. __long i__
6. Neil tried to catch him, but the <u>thief</u> was too fast. __long e__
7. He ran across a <u>field</u> into the woods. __long e__
8. Is this the only crime he ever <u>tried</u>? __long i__
9. I told my friend <u>Frieda</u> about the crime. __long e__
10. The tie thief is a terrible <u>fiend</u>. __long e__
11. The police found a <u>piece</u> of evidence. __long e__
12. They retrieved his <u>handkerchiefs</u> at the scene. __long e__
13. They <u>believe</u> it will help them jail the thief. __long e__
14. The thief didn't <u>achieve</u> much by stealing. __long e__

5

Blue Suitcase

The vowel digraphs **ue** and **ui** often have the sound of long **u**, but not always.

Examples: **long u sound**
ui in suitcase
ue in blue

short i sound
ui as in building

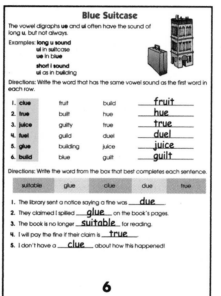

Directions: Write the word that has the same vowel sound as the first word in each row.

1. clue	fruit	build	__fruit__
2. true	built	hue	__hue__
3. juice	guilty	true	__true__
4. fuel	guild	duel	__duel__
5. glue	building	juice	__juice__
6. build	blue	guilt	__guilt__

Directions: Write the word from the box that best completes each sentence.

| suitable | glue | clue | due | true |

1. The library sent a notice saying a fine was __due__.
2. They claimed I spilled __glue__ on the book's pages.
3. The book is no longer __suitable__ for reading.
4. I will pay the fine if their claim is __true__.
5. I don't have a __clue__ about how this happened!

6

Vowel Digraph ea

The vowel digraph **ea** can have the sound of short **e**, long **a**, or long **e**.

Examples: **short e sound**
ea in bread   The [image] has the sound of short **e**.

long a sound
ea in break   The [image] has the sound of long **a**.

long e sound
ea in seat   The [image] has the sound of long **e**.

Directions: Write a word from the box that rhymes with the underlined word.

| dread | beak | beast | steak | bread | meat |
| steady | preacher | mean | seal | break | disease |

1. I enjoyed the characters in the book I just <u>read</u>. __bread or dread__
2. My friend says the characters and events are <u>real</u>. __seal__
3. Let's ask the <u>teacher</u> if this is true. __preacher__
4. We can ask her after the lunch <u>break</u>. __steak__
5. I hope the cafeteria serves something good to <u>eat</u>. __meat__
6. I feel like eating a huge <u>feast</u>. __beast__
7. I like when the meat in the burgers is <u>lean</u>. __mean__
8. Do you wish they would serve <u>steak</u> and potatoes? __break__
9. Are you <u>ready</u> to eat lunch now? __steady__
10. I see our teacher at the <u>head</u> of the lunch line. __dread or bread__
11. Would you <u>please</u> talk to the teacher for me? __disease__
12. Maybe we can <u>speak</u> to her after school instead. __beak__

7

Good Food

The vowel digraph **oo** can have the sound you hear in **good** or **food**.

Examples: cook
spoon

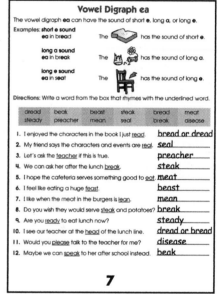

Directions: Write the words from the box under the correct heading.

snooze	book	room	shook
hood	stoop	stood	wool
tooth	took	foot	rooster
loose	droop	crook	proof
cookies	bloom	spool	look

Sound of **oo** as in good
1. __hood__
2. __stood__
3. __took__
4. __wool__
5. __crook__
6. __foot__
7. __book__
8. __cookies__
9. __look__
10. __wood__

Sound of **oo** as in food
11. __droop__
12. __room__
13. __rooster__
14. __bloom__
15. __snooze__
16. __tooth__
17. __spool__
18. __stoop__
19. __proof__
20. __loose__

8

Vowel Digraphs au and aw

The vowel digraphs **au** and **aw** usually have the same sound.

Examples: au
sauce
aw
jaw

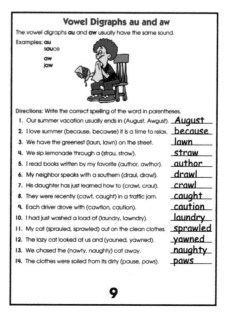

Directions: Write the correct spelling of the word in parentheses.

1. Our summer vacation usually ends in (August, Awgust). __August__
2. I love summer (because, becawse) it is a time to relax. __because__
3. We have the greenest (laun, lawn) on the street. __lawn__
4. We sip lemonade through a (strau, straw). __straw__
5. I read books written by my favorite (author, awthor). __author__
6. My neighbor speaks with a southern (draul, drawl). __drawl__
7. His daughter has just learned how to (crawl, craul). __crawl__
8. They were recently (cawt, caught) in a traffic jam. __caught__
9. Each driver drove with (cawtion, caution). __caution__
10. I had just washed a load of (laundry, lawndry). __laundry__
11. My cat (sprauled, sprawled) out on the clean clothes. __sprawled__
12. The lazy cat looked at us and (yauned, yawned). __yawned__
13. We chased the (nawty, naughty) cat away. __naughty__
14. The clothes were soiled from its dirty (pause, paws). __paws__

9

Diphthongs

Diphthongs are two vowels together that make a new sound.

Examples: **oi**
coin

oy
boy

ew
new

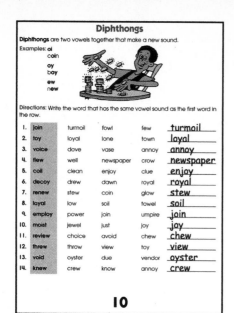

Directions: Write the word that has the same vowel sound as the first word in the row.

1.	join	turmoil	fowl	few	turmoil
2.	toy	loyal	lone	town	loyal
3.	voice	dove	vase	annoy	annoy
4.	flew	well	newspaper	crow	newspaper
5.	coil	clean	enjoy	clue	enjoy
6.	decoy	drew	dawn	royal	royal
7.	renew	stew	coin	glow	stew
8.	loyal	low	soil	towel	soil
9.	employ	power	join	umpire	join
10.	moist	jewel	just	joy	joy
11.	review	choice	avoid	chew	chew
12.	threw	throw	view	toy	view
13.	void	oyster	due	vendor	oyster
14.	knew	crew	know	annoy	crew

10

Out, Now, Brown Cow!

Remember, diphthongs are two vowels together that make a new sound. The diphthongs **ou** and **ow** often have the same sound.

Examples: **ou**
house

ow
flowers

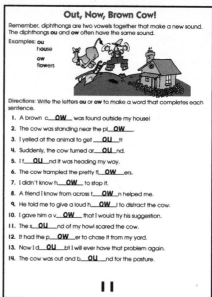

Directions: Write the letters **ou** or **ow** to make a word that completes each sentence.

1. A brown c__OW__ was found outside my house!
2. The cow was standing near the pl__OW__.
3. I yelled at the animal to get __OU__t!
4. Suddenly, the cow turned ar__OU__nd.
5. I f__OU__nd it was heading my way.
6. The cow trampled the pretty fl__OW__ers.
7. I didn't know h__OW__ to stop it.
8. A friend I know from across t__OW__n helped me.
9. He told me to give a loud h__OW__l to distract the cow.
10. I gave him a v__OW__ that I would try his suggestion.
11. The s__OU__nd of my howl scared the cow.
12. It had the p__OW__er to chase it from my yard.
13. Now I d__OU__bt I will ever have that problem again.
14. The cow was out and b__OU__nd for the pasture.

11

Compound Words

Some words are made by putting two different words together. The new word is called a **compound word.**

Example: grape + fruit = grapefruit

Directions: Draw a line to match a word from each column to make a compound word. Write each compound word on a line below.

1. high
2. rail
3. home
4. pea
5. sun
6. base
7. sail
8. side
9. play
10. tooth

shine
work
boat
way
nut
road
walk
brush
ball
ground

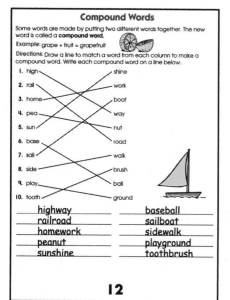

highway
railroad
homework
peanut
sunshine

baseball
sailboat
sidewalk
playground
toothbrush

12

Contractions

Contractions are two words joined into one. When the words are joined, at least one letter is left out. An apostrophe replaces the missing letter or letters.

Examples: I + will
they + are
they + have
has + not
he + would

I'll
they're
they've
hasn't
he'd

Directions: Write a contraction for each pair of words.

1. is not — isn't
4. he is — he's
7. she will — she'll
10. where is — where's

2. she is — she's
5. I would — I'd
8. did not — didn't
11. they would — they'd

3. they have — they've
6. you are — you're
9. he will — he'll
12. she has — she's

13

What's Missing?

they're
it's
she'll
let's
we're
we'll
you're
I'm
that's
I'll
he's
they'll

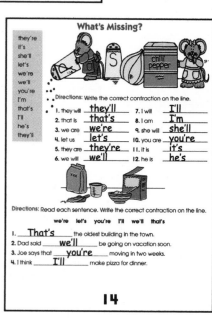

Directions: Write the correct contraction on the line.

1. they will — they'll
2. that is — that's
3. we are — we're
4. let us — let's
5. they are — they're
6. we will — we'll
7. I will — I'll
8. I am — I'm
9. she will — she'll
10. you are — you're
11. it is — it's
12. he is — he's

Directions: Read each sentence. Write the correct contraction on the line.

we're   let's   you're   I'll   we'll   that's

1. __That's__ the oldest building in the town.
2. Dad said __we'll__ be going on vacation soon.
3. Joe says that __you're__ moving in two weeks.
4. I think __I'll__ make pizza for dinner.

14

Letter Ladders

Singular means one, and **plural** means more than one. Add **s** to most nouns to make them plural. Add **es** if the singular noun ends in **s, x, z, ch,** or **sh.**

Directions: Write the plural form of each noun on the correct ladder.

Add s | Add es

banana
whale
patch
orange
wish
class
tiger
flash
scratch
flower
kiss
coin
dish
switch
snake
bus
hoop
tax
key
trail

Add s:
bananas
whales
oranges
tigers
flowers
coins
snakes
hoops
keys
trails

Add es:
patches
wishes
classes
flashes
scratches
kisses
dishes
switches
buses
taxes

15

Plural Endings

Remember, singular means one, and plural means more than one. When a singular noun ends in a consonant and **y,** change the **y** to **i** and add **es.**

Example: candy   candies

Some singular nouns form plurals with special spellings. You need to memorize them.

Examples: man — men
woman — women
child — children
foot — feet
tooth — teeth
mouse — mice

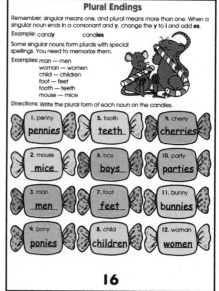

Directions: Write the plural form of each noun on the candies.

1. penny — pennies
2. mouse — mice
3. man — men
4. pony — ponies
5. tooth — teeth
6. boy — boys
7. foot — feet
8. child — children
9. cherry — cherries
10. party — parties
11. bunny — bunnies
12. woman — women

16

Building Words

One way to build a new word is to add a prefix to the beginning of a word. A **prefix** is a word part added to the beginning of a word that changes the meaning of the word.

Examples:

prefix	+	word	=	new word	Prefix Meaning
re	+	place	=	replace	(again)
un	+	even	=	uneven	(not)
mid	+	air	=	midair	(middle)
in	+	accurate	=	inaccurate	(not)

Directions: Write a new word for each meaning using a prefix from above.

1. paint again — repaint
2. not fair — unfair
3. not complete — incomplete
4. the middle of the day — midday
5. not touched — untouched
6. write again — rewrite
7. not clear — unclear
8. do again — redo
9. not direct — indirect
10. not fit — unfit
11. wrap again — rewrap
12. the middle of summer — midsummer
13. not true — untrue
14. read again — reread
15. the middle of a stream — midstream
16. not expensive — inexpensive

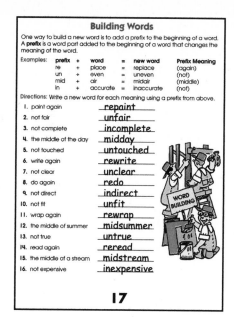

17

Suffixes

Another way to build a new word is to add a suffix to the end of the word. A **suffix** is a word part that is added to the end of a word to change its meaning.

Examples:

word	+	suffix	=	new word	(suffix meaning)
sing	+	er	=	singer	(a person or thing)
care	+	less	=	careless	(without)
skill	+	ful	=	skillful	(full of)

er	less	ful

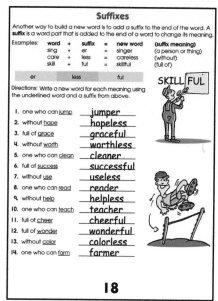

Directions: Write a new word for each meaning using the underlined word and a suffix from above.

1. one who can jump — jumper
2. without hope — hopeless
3. full of grace — graceful
4. without worth — worthless
5. one who can clean — cleaner
6. full of success — successful
7. without use — useless
8. one who can read — reader
9. without help — helpless
10. one who can teach — teacher
11. full of cheer — cheerful
12. full of wonder — wonderful
13. without color — colorless
14. one who can farm — farmer

18

Base Words

A word without any prefixes or suffixes is called a **base word** or **root word**. Prefixes and suffixes change a base word's meaning.

Example: The base word in de**frost**ed is **frost**. The prefix is **de** and the suffix is **ed**.

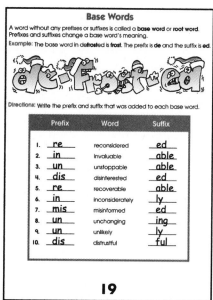

Directions: Write the prefix and suffix that was added to each base word.

	Prefix	Word	Suffix
1.	re	reconsidered	ed
2.	in	invaluable	able
3.	un	unstoppable	able
4.	dis	disinterested	ed
5.	re	recoverable	able
6.	in	inconsiderately	ly
7.	mis	misinformed	ed
8.	un	unchanging	ing
9.	un	unlikely	ly
10.	dis	distrustful	ful

19

The Root of the Problem

Directions: Underline the root of each word in the list. Then, circle the root words in the word search. Words may go up, down, across, backwards, and diagonally.

1. planting
2. mending
3. fishing
4. golden
5. swimming
6. certainly
7. suddenly
8. arrows
9. foolish
10. sounds
11. sighing
12. rushing
13. safely
14. asleep
15. longer
16. arms
17. stones
18. bandits

```
A P L A N T H S I F
R O C E R T A I N O
M E N D D N U O S O
I A E L P R E K I L
W R D O G N J O L G
S R D G O R U S H F
N O U T S L E E P A
V W S T I D N A B S
```

20

Syllables

A **syllable** is a smaller part of a word that has a vowel sound. The number of syllables is the number of vowel sounds you hear.

Examples: mouse — **1** syllable
afraid — **2** syllables
stepmother — **3** syllables

To help you say a longer word, you can divide it into syllables . . .

between two consonants — hap/py
after a long vowel — o/pen
after the consonant when the vowel is short — cab/in
to separate prefixes and suffixes — mis/treat/ment

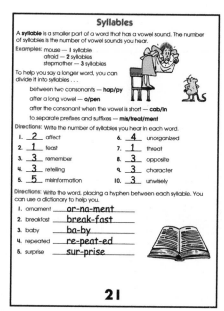

Directions: Write the number of syllables you hear in each word.

1. 2 affect
2. 1 feast
3. 3 remember
4. 3 retelling
5. 5 misinformation
6. 4 unorganized
7. 1 threat
8. 3 opposite
9. 3 character
10. 3 unwisely

Directions: Write the word, placing a hyphen between each syllable. You can use a dictionary to help you.

1. ornament — or-na-ment
2. breakfast — break-fast
3. baby — ba-by
4. repeated — re-peat-ed
5. surprise — sur-prise

21

Quilting Bee

Directions: Follow the code to color the quilt squares.

1-syllable words = blue	3-syllable words = green
2-syllable words = red	4-syllable words = yellow

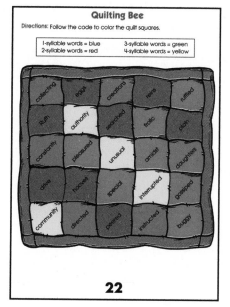

22

Circle a Synonym

Words that mean the same thing, or almost the same thing, are called **synonyms**.

Directions: Circle a synonym for the **boldfaced** word in each line. Then, select another synonym from the word list to write in the blanks.

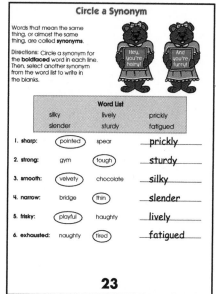

Word List		
silky	lively	prickly
slender	sturdy	fatigued

1. sharp: (pointed) spear — prickly
2. strong: gym (tough) — sturdy
3. smooth: (velvety) chocolate — silky
4. narrow: bridge (thin) — slender
5. frisky: (playful) haughty — lively
6. exhausted: naughty (tired) — fatigued

23

Synonym Snob!

Sydney is a synonym snob! She hates to use the same words as everybody else. Help Sydney say her student council speech using super synonyms! Change each underlined word to a more exciting synonym. You may use the word list below for ideas.

Word List

brainy	balmy	incredibly	bright
good	luminous	outrageously	kind
morning	superb	hello	polite
attend	fantastic	clever	elect
humid	hot	intelligent	orderly
pleasant	extremely	prepared	wonderful

<u>Hi</u>, my name is Sydney. I <u>go to</u> Aloha School in <u>warm</u> and <u>sunny</u> Hawaii. I would like to be on student council because I can do a <u>great</u> job. I am <u>very</u> <u>smart</u>, and I work hard. Also, I am very <u>organized</u> and <u>nice</u> to people. Those are the reasons you should <u>vote for</u> me!

Directions: Write Sydney's new speech on the lines below:

Answers will vary.

24

Antonyms Are Opposites

Words with opposite meanings are called **antonyms**.
Directions: Circle the pair of antonyms in each box. Complete each sentence with one of the circled words.

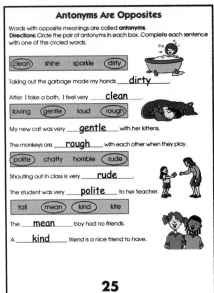

(clean) shine sparkle (dirty)

Taking out the garbage made my hands __dirty__ .

After I take a bath, I feel very __clean__ .

loving (gentle) loud (rough)

My new cat was very __gentle__ with her kittens.

The monkeys are __rough__ with each other when they play.

(polite) chatty horrible (rude)

Shouting out in class is very __rude__ .

The student was very __polite__ to her teacher.

tall (mean) (kind) kite

The __mean__ boy had no friends.

A __kind__ friend is a nice friend to have.

25

Antonyms Puzzle

Directions: Fill in the crossword puzzle below. Use the clues in the word list, except choose each word's **opposite** meaning. Good luck!

Word List

Across	Down
1. above	2. win
4. full	3. laugh
6. messy	5. war
8. easy	7. loose
9. serious	8. wet

```
B E L O W
O
S   C
E M P T Y   R
A       Y
C
N E A T
    I
    G
D I F F I C U L T
    R
F U N N Y
```

26

Homophones

Words that are pronounced the same, but have different spellings and different meanings, are called **homophones**.

Examples: pear — pair   ate — eight

Directions: Write the correct homophone to complete each sentence.

1. (red / read)
   I __read__ the book.
   My book is __red__ .

2. (pear / pair / pare)
   I ate the delicious __pear__ .
   I have a __pair__ of gloves.
   Will you __pare__ the fruit?

3. (sun / son)
   They have a polite __son__ .
   The __sun__ is shining today.

4. (ate / eight)
   I __ate__ pizza for lunch.
   I bought __eight__ pens.

5. (way / weigh)
   How much do you __weigh__ ?
   Do you know the __way__ there?

6. (to / two / too)
   We have __two__ apples.
   We went __to__ the store.
   I have an apple, __too__ .

7. (one / won)
   I __won__ the race.
   I have __one__ brother.

8. (I / eye)
   Dust blew into my __eye__ .
   __I__ blinked to get rid of it.

Directions: Circle the homophone that names the picture.

1. not (knot)   2. (hour) our   3. (board) bored   4. due (dew)

27

Be a Busy Bee

Directions: Underline the correct homophone for each sentence.

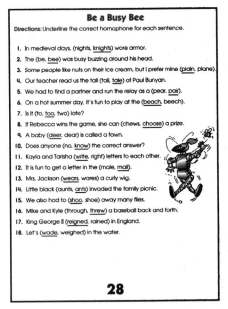

1. In medieval days, (nights, <u>knights</u>) wore armor.
2. The (be, <u>bee</u>) was busy buzzing around his head.
3. Some people like nuts on their ice cream, but I prefer mine (<u>plain</u>, plane).
4. Our teacher read us the tall (tail, <u>tale</u>) of Paul Bunyan.
5. We had to find a partner and run the relay as a (pear, <u>pair</u>).
6. On a hot summer day, it's fun to play at the (<u>beach</u>, beech).
7. Is it (to, <u>too</u>, two) late?
8. If Rebecca wins the game, she can (chews, <u>choose</u>) a prize.
9. A baby (<u>deer</u>, dear) is called a fawn.
10. Does anyone (no, <u>know</u>) the correct answer?
11. Kayla and Tarisha (<u>write</u>, right) letters to each other.
12. It is fun to get a letter in the (male, <u>mail</u>).
13. Mrs. Jackson (<u>wears</u>, wares) a curly wig.
14. Little black (aunts, <u>ants</u>) invaded the family picnic.
15. We also had to (<u>shoo</u>, shoe) away many flies.
16. Mike and Kyle (through, <u>threw</u>) a baseball back and forth.
17. King George II (<u>reigned</u>, rained) in England.
18. Let's (<u>wade</u>, weighed) in the water.

28

Nouns

Nouns are words that tell the names of people, places, or things.

Directions: Read the words below. Then, write them in the correct column.

goat	Mrs. Jackson	girl
beach	tree	song
mouth	park	Jean Rivers
finger	flower	New York
Kevin Jones	Elm City	Frank Gates
Main Street	theater	skates
River Park	father	boy

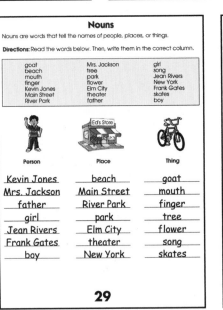

Person	Place	Thing
Kevin Jones	beach	goat
Mrs. Jackson	Main Street	mouth
father	River Park	finger
girl	park	tree
Jean Rivers	Elm City	flower
Frank Gates	theater	song
boy	New York	skates

29

Common Nouns

Common nouns are nouns that name any member of a group of people, places, or things, rather than specific people, places, or things.

Directions: Read the sentences below and write the common noun found in each sentence.

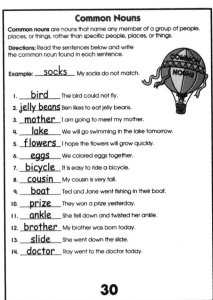

Example: __socks__ My socks do not match.

1. __bird__ The bird could not fly.
2. __jelly beans__ Ben likes to eat jelly beans.
3. __mother__ I am going to meet my mother.
4. __lake__ We will go swimming in the lake tomorrow.
5. __flowers__ I hope the flowers will grow quickly.
6. __eggs__ We colored eggs together.
7. __bicycle__ It is easy to ride a bicycle.
8. __cousin__ My cousin is very tall.
9. __boat__ Ted and Jane went fishing in their boat.
10. __prize__ They won a prize yesterday.
11. __ankle__ She fell down and twisted her ankle.
12. __brother__ My brother was born today.
13. __slide__ She went down the slide.
14. __doctor__ Ray went to the doctor today.

30

Proper Nouns

Proper nouns are names of specific people, places, or things. Proper nouns begin with a capital letter.

Directions: Read the sentences below and circle the proper nouns found in each sentence.

Example: (Aunt Frances) gave me a puppy for my birthday.

1. We lived on (Jackson Street) before we moved to our new house.
2. (Angela's) birthday party is tomorrow night.
3. We drove through (Cheyenne, Wyoming,) on our way home.
4. (Dr. Charles) always gives me a treat for not crying.
5. (George Washington) was our first president.
6. Our class took a field trip to the (Johnson Flower Farm.)
7. (Uncle Jack) lives in (New York City.)
8. (Amy) and (Elizabeth) are best friends.
9. We buy doughnuts at the (Grayson Bakery.)
10. My favorite movie is (E.T.)
11. We flew to (Miami, Florida,) in a plane.
12. We go to (Riverfront Stadium) to watch the baseball games.
13. (Mr. Fields) is a wonderful music teacher.
14. My best friend is (Tom Dunlap.)

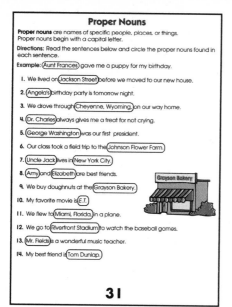

31

Little Words Mean a Lot

A **pronoun** is a word that takes the place of a noun.

Directions: Above each **bold** word below, write a pronoun that could replace it.

| she | it | her | we | he | his | I | him | they | your |

1. Uncle Nick shouted at Mus Mus as **Uncle Nick** [he] walked to the kitchen.
2. **Lucy** [She] ran to **Lucy's** [her] mother in tears.
3. **The Littles** [They] crowded up to the kitchen door.
4. Granny Little said, "**Granny Little** [I] wouldn't believe it if **Granny Little** [I] didn't see it with these old eyes."
5. Lucy said, "**Mus Mus** [It] is a cute name.
6. **Will and Tom** [They] have gone to get some leftovers.
7. Uncle Nick kept on writing **Uncle Nick's** [his] life story.
8. Mrs. Little whispered, "Don't bother **Uncle Nick** [him]."
9. Granny Little turned **Granny Little's** [her] back on **Uncle Nick** [him].
10. Tom told Uncle Nick, "**Lucy and Tom** [They] want to read **Uncle Nick's** [his] book."

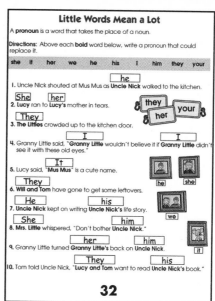

32

Pronouns

Singular Pronouns
I me my mine
you your yours
he she it her
hers his its him

Plural Pronouns
we us our ours
you your yours
they them their theirs

Directions: Underline the pronouns in each sentence.

1. Mom told <u>us</u> to wash <u>our</u> hands.
2. Did <u>you</u> go to the store?
3. <u>We</u> should buy <u>him</u> a present.
4. <u>I</u> called <u>you</u> about <u>their</u> party.
5. <u>Our</u> house had damage on <u>its</u> roof.
6. <u>They</u> want to give <u>you</u> a prize at <u>our</u> party.
7. <u>My</u> cat ate <u>her</u> sandwich.
8. <u>Your</u> coat looks like <u>his</u> coat.

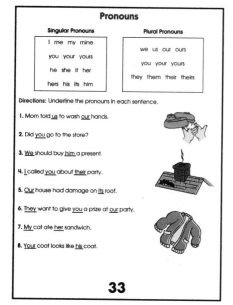

33

Possessive Nouns

Directions: Circle the correct possessive noun for each sentence and write it in the blank.

Example: One ___girl's___ mother is a teacher.
(girl's)   girls'

1. The ___cat's___ tail is long.
(cat's)   cats
2. One ___boy's___ baseball bat is aluminum.
(boy's)   boys
3. The ___waitresses'___ aprons are white.
(waitresses')   waitress's
4. My ___grandmother's___ apple pie is the best!
(grandmother's)   grandmothers'
5. My five ___brothers'___ uniforms are dirty.
brother's   (brothers')
6. The ___child's___ doll is pretty.
(child's)   childs
7. These ___dogs'___ collars are different colors.
dog's   (dogs')
8. The ___cow's___ tail is short.
(cow's)   cows

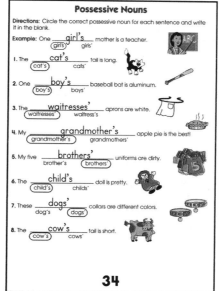

34

Possessive Pronouns

Possessive pronouns show ownership.
Example: his hat, her shoes, our dog

We can use these pronouns before a noun:
my, our, you, his, her, its, their
Example: That is **my** bike.

We can use these pronouns on their own:
mine, yours, ours, his, hers, theirs, its
Example: That is mine.

Directions: Write each sentence again, using a pronoun instead of the words in bold letters. Be sure to use capitals and periods.

Example:
My **dog's** bowl is brown.   **Its** bowl is brown.

1. That is **Lisa's** book.   That is her book.
2. This is **my** pencil.   This is mine.
3. This hat is **your** hat.   This hat is yours.
4. Fifi is **Kevin's** cat.   Fifi is his cat.
5. That beautiful house is **our** home.
   That beautiful house is ours.
6. The **gerbil's** cage is too small.
   Its cage is too small.

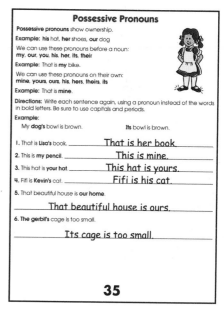

35

Articles "A" and "An"

An **article** is a word that points out a singular noun in a sentence.
Use the article **a** before words beginning with consonants.
Examples: I saw **a** bird fly into a tree.
The bird was building **a** nest.
Use the article **an** before words beginning with vowels or vowel sounds.
Examples: **An** eagle perched on a branch.
There was **an** egg in its nest.

Directions: Write the correct article, **a** or **an**, on the line.

1. I have __an__ aunt named Mary.
2. We went to __a__ movie last night.
3. Mark wrote __a__ long letter.
4. We took __an__ English test.
5. Ned has __an__ old bicycle.
6. We had __an__ ice-cream cone.
7. Maggie ate __an__ orange for breakfast.
8. They saw __a__ deer on their trip.
9. Steve thought the car was __an__ ugly color.
10. Emily bought __a__ new pair of skates.
11. He was __an__ officer in the army.
12. __An__ elephant is such a large animal.
13. Arizona is __a__ state in the Southwest.
14. Rosa was __an__ infielder on her softball team.
15. Jordan ate __an__ apricot for a snack.

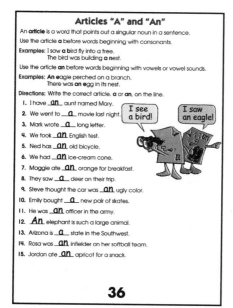

I see a bird!   I saw an eagle!

36

Verbs

A **verb** is a word that can show action. A verb can also tell what someone or something is or is like.

Examples: The boats **sail** on Lake Michigan.
We **eat** dinner at 6:00.
I **am** ten years old.
The clowns **were** funny.

Directions: Circle the verb in each sentence.

1. John (sips) milk.
2. They (throw) the football.
3. We (hiked) in the woods.
4. I (enjoy) music.
5. My friend (smiles) often.
6. A lion (hunts) for food.
7. We (ate) lunch at noon.
8. Fish (swim) in the ocean.
9. My team (won) the game.
10. They (were) last in line.
11. The wind (howled) during the night.
12. Kangaroos (live) in Australia.
13. The plane (flew) into the clouds.
14. We (recorded) the song.
15. They (forgot) the directions.

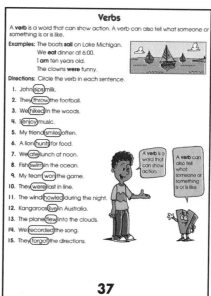

A verb is a word that can show action.
A verb can also tell what someone or something is or is like.

37

Verbs

When a verb tells what one person or thing is doing now, it usually ends in **s**.
Example: She sings.

When a verb is used with **you**, **I**, or **we**, we do not add an **s**.
Example: I sing.

Directions: Write the correct verb in each sentence.

Example:

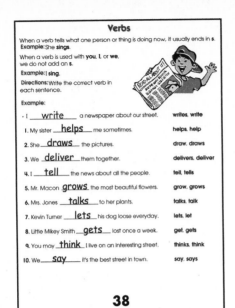

· I __write__ a newspaper about our street. — writes, write

1. My sister __helps__ me sometimes. — helps, help

2. She __draws__ the pictures. — draw, draws

3. We __deliver__ them together. — delivers, deliver

4. I __tell__ the news about all the people. — tell, tells

5. Mr. Macon __grows__ the most beautiful flowers. — grow, grows

6. Mrs. Jones __talks__ to her plants. — talks, talk

7. Kevin Turner __lets__ his dog loose everyday. — lets, let

8. Little Mikey Smith __gets__ lost once a week. — get, gets

9. You may __think__ I live on an interesting street. — thinks, think

10. We __say__ it's the best street in town. — say, says

38

Irregular Verbs

Past-tense verbs that are not formed by adding **ed** are called **irregular verbs**.

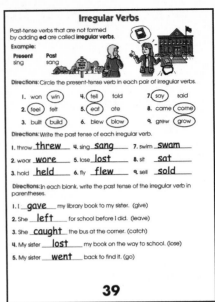

Example:

Present	Past
sing	sang

Directions: Circle the present-tense verb in each pair of irregular verbs.

1. won (win)   4. (tell) told   7. (say) said
2. (feel) felt   5. (eat) ate   8. came (come)
3. built (build) 6. blew (blow)   9. grew (grow)

Directions: Write the past tense of each irregular verb.

1. throw __threw__   4. sing __sang__   7. swim __swam__
2. wear __wore__   5. lose __lost__   8. sit __sat__
3. hold __held__   6. fly __flew__   9. sell __sold__

Directions: In each blank, write the past tense of the irregular verb in parentheses.

1. I __gave__ my library book to my sister. (give)

2. She __left__ for school before I did. (leave)

3. She __caught__ the bus at the corner. (catch)

4. My sister __lost__ my book on the way to school. (lose)

5. My sister __went__ back to find it. (go)

39

Irregular Verbs

The verb **be** is different from all other verbs. The present-tense forms of **be** are **am**, **is**, and **are**. The past-tense forms of **be** are **was** and **were**. The verb **to be** is written in the following ways:

singular: I am, you are, he is, she is, it is
plural: we are, you are, they are

Directions: Choose the correct form of **be** from the words in the box and write it in each sentence. Some sentences may have more than one correct form of **be**.

| are | am | is | was | were |

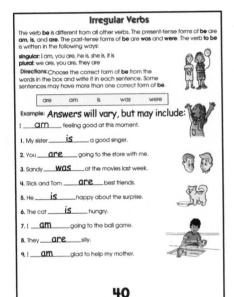

Example: Answers will vary, but may include:

I __am__ feeling good at this moment.

1. My sister __is__ a good singer.

2. You __are__ going to the store with me.

3. Sandy __was__ at the movies last week.

4. Rick and Tom __are__ best friends.

5. He __is__ happy about the surprise.

6. The cat __is__ hungry.

7. I __am__ going to the ball game.

8. They __are__ silly.

9. I __am__ glad to help my mother.

40

Helping Verbs

A **helping verb** is a word used with an action verb.

Examples: might, shall, and are

Directions: Write a helping verb from the box with each action verb.

can	could	must	might
may	would	should	will
shall	did	does	do
had	have	has	am
are	were	is	
be	being	been	

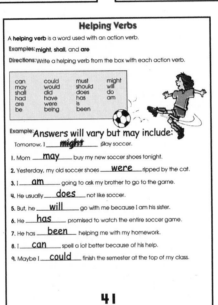

Example: Answers will vary but may include:

Tomorrow, I __might__ play soccer.

1. Mom __may__ buy my new soccer shoes tonight.

2. Yesterday, my old soccer shoes __were__ ripped by the cat.

3. I __am__ going to ask my brother to go to the game.

4. He usually __does__ not like soccer.

5. But, he __will__ go with me because I am his sister.

6. He __has__ promised to watch the entire soccer game.

7. He has __been__ helping me with my homework.

8. I __can__ spell a lot better because of his help.

9. Maybe I __could__ finish the semester at the top of my class.

41

Linking Verbs

A **linking verb** does not show action. Instead, it links the subject of the sentence with a noun or adjective in the predicate. **Am**, **is**, **are**, **was**, and **were** are linking verbs.

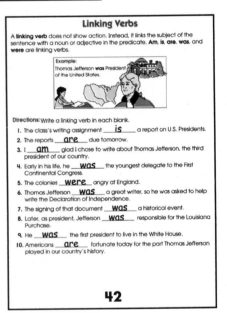

Example:
Thomas Jefferson **was** President of the United States.

Directions: Write a linking verb in each blank.

1. The class's writing assignment __is__ a report on U.S. Presidents.

2. The reports __are__ due tomorrow.

3. I __am__ glad I chose to write about Thomas Jefferson, the third president of our country.

4. Early in his life, he __was__ the youngest delegate to the First Continental Congress.

5. The colonies __were__ angry at England.

6. Thomas Jefferson __was__ a great writer, so he was asked to help write the Declaration of Independence.

7. The signing of that document __was__ a historical event.

8. Later, as president, Jefferson __was__ responsible for the Louisiana Purchase.

9. He __was__ the first president to live in the White House.

10. Americans __are__ fortunate today for the part Thomas Jefferson played in our country's history.

42

Review

Verb tenses can be in the past, present, or future.

Directions: Match each sentence with the correct verb tense. (Think: When did each thing happen?)

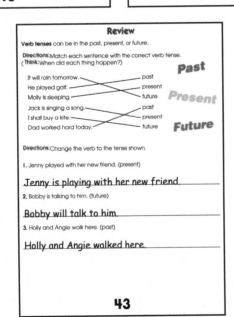

It will rain tomorrow. — past
He played golf. — present
Molly is sleeping. — future

Jack is singing a song. — past
I shall buy a kite. — present
Dad worked hard today. — future

Past
Present
Future

Directions: Change the verb to the tense shown.

1. Jenny played with her new friend. (present)

Jenny is playing with her new friend.

2. Bobby is talking to him. (future)

Bobby will talk to him.

3. Holly and Angie walk here. (past)

Holly and Angie walked here.

43

Marvelous Modifiers

Words that describe are called **adjectives**.
Directions: Circle the adjectives in the sentences below.

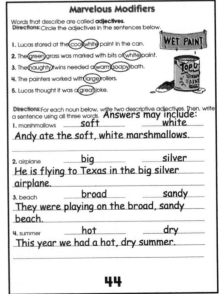

1. Lucas stared at the (cool) (white) paint in the can.
2. The (green) grass was marked with bits of (white) paint.
3. The (naughty) twins needed a (warm) (soapy) bath.
4. The painters worked with (large) rollers.
5. Lucas thought it was a (great) joke.

Directions: For each noun below, write two descriptive adjectives. Then, write a sentence using all three words. **Answers may include:**

1. marshmallows __soft__ __white__
Andy ate the soft, white marshmallows.

2. airplane __big__ __silver__
He is flying to Texas in the big silver airplane.

3. beach __broad__ __sandy__
They were playing on the broad, sandy beach.

4. summer __hot__ __dry__
This year we had a hot, dry summer.

44

---

76 *Reading: Grade 3*

Adverbs

An **adverb** is a word that can describe a verb. It tells how, when, or where an action takes place.

Example:
The snow fell **quietly**. (how)
It snowed **yesterday**. (when)
It fell **everywhere**. (where)

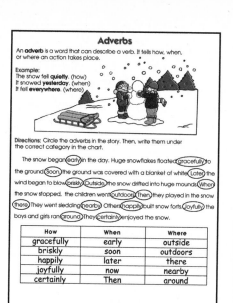

Directions: Circle the adverbs in the story. Then, write them under the correct category in the chart.

The snow began (early) in the day. Huge snowflakes floated (gracefully) to the ground. (Soon) the ground was covered with a blanket of white. (Later) the wind began to blow (briskly). (Outside,) the snow drifted into huge mounds. (When) the snow stopped, the children went (outdoors). (Then) they played in the snow (there). They went sledding (nearby). Others (happily) built snow forts. (Joyfully) the boys and girls ran (around). They (certainly) enjoyed the snow.

How	When	Where
gracefully	early	outside
briskly	soon	outdoors
happily	later	there
joyfully	now	nearby
certainly	Then	around

45

Adjectives and Adverbs

An **adjective** is used to describe a noun. An **adverb** describes a verb or an action.

Example:
We went into the **busy** pet store. (adjective)
Dad and I walked **quickly** through the mall. (adverb)

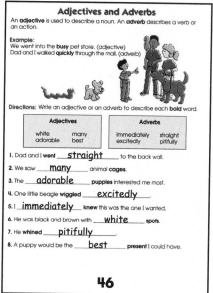

Directions: Write an adjective or an adverb to describe each **bold** word.

Adjectives		Adverbs	
white	many	immediately	straight
adorable	best	excitedly	pitifully

1. Dad and I **went** __straight__ to the back wall.
2. We saw __many__ animal **cages**.
3. The __adorable__ **puppies** interested me most.
4. One little beagle **wiggled** __excitedly__.
5. I __immediately__ **knew** this was the one I wanted.
6. He was black and brown with __white__ **spots**.
7. He **whined** __pitifully__.
8. A puppy would be the __best__ **present** I could have.

46

Commas

Commas are used to separate words in a series of three or more.

Example: My favorite fruits are apples, bananas, and oranges.

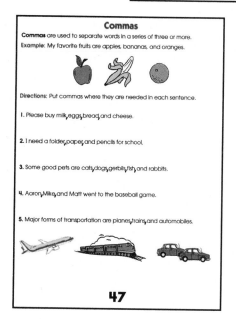

Directions: Put commas where they are needed in each sentence.

1. Please buy milk, eggs, bread, and cheese.

2. I need a folder, paper, and pencils for school.

3. Some good pets are cats, dogs, gerbils, fish, and rabbits.

4. Aaron, Mike, and Matt went to the baseball game.

5. Major forms of transportation are planes, trains, and automobiles.

47

Articles and Commas

Directions: Write **a** or **an** in each blank. Put commas where they are needed in the paragraphs below.

Owls

__An__ owl is __a__ bird of prey. This means it hunts small animals. Owls catch insects, fish and birds. Mice are __an__ owl's favorite dinner. Owls like protected places, such as trees, burrows or barns. Owls make noises that sound like hoots, screeches or even barks. __An__ owl's feathers may be black, brown, gray or white.

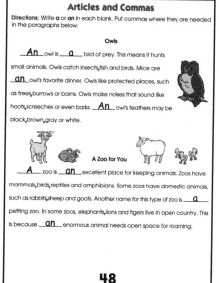

A Zoo for You

__A__ zoo is __an__ excellent place for keeping animals. Zoos have mammals, birds, reptiles and amphibians. Some zoos have domestic animals, such as rabbits, sheep and goats. Another name for this type of zoo is __a__ petting zoo. In some zoos, elephants, lions and tigers live in open country. This is because __an__ enormous animal needs open space for roaming.

48

Subjects and Predicates

Every sentence has two parts. The **subject** tells who or what the sentence is about. The **predicate** tells what the subject does, did, is, or has.

Example: The snowman is melting.
        subject   predicate

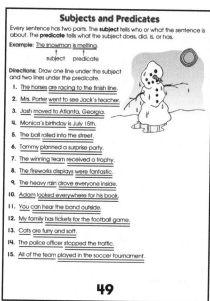

Directions: Draw one line under the subject and two lines under the predicate.

1. The horses are racing to the finish line.
2. Mrs. Porter went to see Jack's teacher.
3. Josh moved to Atlanta, Georgia.
4. Monica's birthday is July 15th.
5. The ball rolled into the street.
6. Tammy planned a surprise party.
7. The winning team received a trophy.
8. The fireworks displays were fantastic.
9. The heavy rain drove everyone inside.
10. Adam looked everywhere for his book.
11. You can hear the band outside.
12. My family has tickets for the football game.
13. Cats are furry and soft.
14. The police officer stopped the traffic.
15. All of the team played in the soccer tournament.

49

Making Sentences

Remember, a sentence must tell a complete thought.

Directions: Draw a line from each beginning to an ending that makes a complete sentence.

1. John and Patty attend — for two fun-filled weeks.
2. The band camp lasts — and Patty plays the flute.
3. All the kids bring — practice music together.
4. John plays the clarinet — a band camp every summer.
5. Each day the kids — they give a final concert.
6. The teacher helps them — improve their performance.
7. On the last day, — their own instruments.

50

Sentence Building

A **sentence** can tell more and more.

Directions: Read the sentence parts. Write a word on each line to make each sentence tell more.

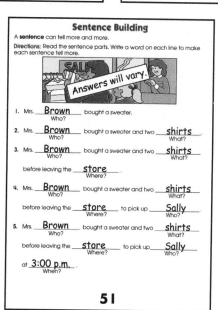
Answers will vary.

1. Mrs. __Brown__ bought a sweater.
   Who?

2. Mrs. __Brown__ bought a sweater and two __shirts__.
   Who?   What?

3. Mrs. __Brown__ bought a sweater and two __shirts__
   Who?   What?
   before leaving the __store__.
                   Where?

4. Mrs. __Brown__ bought a sweater and two __shirts__
   Who?   What?
   before leaving the __store__ to pick up __Sally__.
                   Where?   Who?

5. Mrs. __Brown__ bought a sweater and two __shirts__
   Who?   What?
   before leaving the __store__ to pick up __Sally__
                   Where?   Who?
   at __3:00 p.m.__
      When?

51

Paragraph Form

A **paragraph** is a group of sentences about one main idea. When writing a paragraph, remember these rules:

1. **Indent** the first line.
2. **Capitalize** the first word of each sentence.
3. **Punctuate** each sentence.

Directions: Rewrite each paragraph correctly by following the three rules.

the number of teeth you have depends on your age a baby has no teeth at all gradually, milk teeth, or baby teeth, begin to grow later, these teeth fall out and permanent teeth appear by the age of twenty-five, you should have thirty-two permanent teeth.

The number of teeth you have depends on your age. A baby has no teeth at all. Gradually, milk teeth, or baby teeth, begin to grow. Later, these teeth fall out and permanent teeth appear. By the age of twenty-five, you should have thirty-two permanent teeth.

my family is going to Disneyland tomorrow we plan to arrive early my dad will take my little sister to Fantasyland first meanwhile, my brother and I will visit Frontierland and Adventureland after lunch, we will all meet to go to Tomorrowland

My family is going to Disneyland tomorrow. We plan to arrive early. My dad will take my little sister to Fantasyland first. Meanwhile, my brother and I will visit Frontierland and Adventureland. After lunch, we will all meet to go to Tomorrowland.

52

Topic Sentences

Remember, a paragraph is a group of sentences that tells about one main idea. One of the sentences states the main idea. That sentence is called the **topic sentence**. The topic sentence is often the first sentence in the paragraph.

Example:
Three planets in our solar system have rings around them. The planets with rings are Saturn, Uranus, and Jupiter. The rings are actually thin belts of rocks that orbit the planets. Saturn is the most famous ringed planet.

Directions: Underline the topic sentence in the paragraph below.

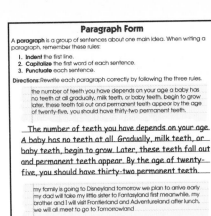

Every weekday morning, I follow a basic routine to get ready for school. I get up about 7 A.M., wash my face, and get dressed. Then, I eat breakfast and brush my teeth. Finally, I pack my books and walk to the bus stop.

Directions: Write a topic sentence for a paragraph about each idea.

1. Homework: _____
2. Breakfast: _____
3. Neighbors: _____
4. Friends: _____
5. Camping: _____

Answers will vary.

53

Support Sentences

Remember, the topic sentence gives the main idea of a paragraph. The **support sentences** give details about the main idea. Each support sentence must relate to the main idea.

Directions: Underline the topic sentence in the paragraph. Cross out the sentence that is not a support sentence. Write another to replace it.

Throwing a surprise birthday party can be exciting but tricky. The honored person must not hear a word about the party! On the day of the party, everyone should arrive early. A snack may ruin your appetite. _____

Directions: Write two support sentences to go with each topic sentence.

1. Giving a dog a bath can be a real challenge!
   A. _____
   B. _____
2. I can still remember how much fun we had that _____
   A. _____
   B. _____
3. Sometimes I like to imagine _____ historic world was like.
   A. _____
   B. _____
4. A daily newspa_____ atures many kinds of news.
   A. _____
   B. _____

Answers will vary.

54

Paragraph Plan

Directions: Follow the paragraph plan described on the previous page.

A Day to Remember   Being a Good Friend   Staying Healthy

Step 1: Topic _____
Step 2: Ideas _____
_____
_____
Step 3: Topic Sentence _____
Step 4: Support Sentences _____
_____
_____
Step 5: Write Paragraph _____
_____
_____
_____

Answers will vary.

56

Step-by-Step Car Wash

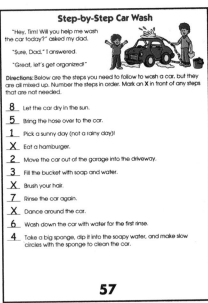

"Hey, Tim! Will you help me wash the car today?" asked my dad.

"Sure, Dad," I answered.

"Great, let's get organized!"

Directions: Below are the steps you need to follow to wash a car, but they are all mixed up. Number the steps in order. Mark an **X** in front of any steps that are not needed.

- **8** Let the car dry in the sun.
- **5** Bring the hose over to the car.
- **1** Pick a sunny day (not a rainy day)!
- **X** Eat a hamburger.
- **2** Move the car out of the garage into the driveway.
- **3** Fill the bucket with soap and water.
- **X** Brush your hair.
- **7** Rinse the car again.
- **X** Dance around the car.
- **6** Wash down the car with water for the first rinse.
- **4** Take a big sponge, dip it into the soapy water, and make slow circles with the sponge to clean the car.

57

State Search

Following directions means reading and doing exactly what the words say to do.

Directions: Follow the directions below the list of places. Then, put a check in the box after you complete each direction.

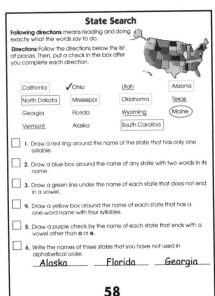

California	✓ Ohio	Utah	Arizona
North Dakota	Mississippi	Oklahoma	Texas
Georgia	Florida	Wyoming	(Maine)
Vermont	Alaska	South Carolina	

☐ 1. Draw a red ring around the name of the state that has only one syllable.
☐ 2. Draw a blue box around the name of any state with two words in its name.
☐ 3. Draw a green line under the name of each state that does not end in a vowel.
☐ 4. Draw a yellow box around the name of each state that has a one-word name with four syllables.
☐ 5. Draw a purple check by the name of each state that ends with a vowel other than **a** or **e**.
☐ 6. Write the names of three states that you have not used in alphabetical order.

  Alaska   Florida   Georgia

58

Main Message

The **main idea** is the most important idea about a topic, or the message a writer wants you to understand.

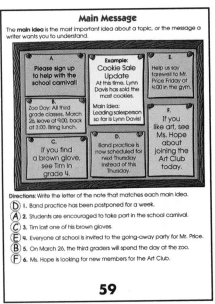

A. Please sign up to help with the school carnival!

Example: Cookie Sale Update — At this time, Lynn Davis has sold the most cookies. Main Idea: Leading salesperson so far is Lynn Davis!

E. Help us say farewell to Mr. Price Friday at 4:00 in the gym.

B. Zoo Day: All third grade classes, March 26, leave at 9:00, back at 3:00. Bring lunch.

F. If you like art, see Ms. Hope about joining the Art Club today.

C. If you find a brown glove, see Tim in grade 4.

D. Band practice is now scheduled for next Thursday instead of this Thursday.

Directions: Write the letter of the note that matches each main idea.

- (D) 1. Band practice has been postponed for a week.
- (A) 2. Students are encouraged to take part in the school carnival.
- (C) 3. Tim lost one of his brown gloves.
- (E) 4. Everyone at school is invited to the going-away party for Mr. Price.
- (B) 5. On March 26, the third graders will spend the day at the zoo.
- (F) 6. Ms. Hope is looking for new members for the Art Club.

59

Get the Point

The main idea can be the point or purpose of the entire story. Also, each paragraph within a story may have its own main idea.

Directions: Read the story. Then, write an **X** next to each correct main idea.

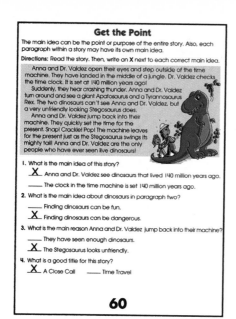

Anna and Dr. Valdez open their eyes and step outside of the time machine. They have landed in the middle of a jungle. Dr. Valdez checks the time clock. It is set at 140 million years ago!

Suddenly, they hear crashing thunder. Anna and Dr. Valdez turn around and see a giant Apatosaurus and a Tyrannosaurus Rex. The two dinosaurs can't see Anna and Dr. Valdez, but a very unfriendly looking Stegosaurus does.

Anna and Dr. Valdez jump back into their machine. They quickly set the time for the present. Snap! Crackle! Pop! The machine leaves for the present just as the Stegosaurus swings its mighty tail. Anna and Dr. Valdez are the only people who have ever seen live dinosaurs!

1. What is the main idea of this story?

  __X__ Anna and Dr. Valdez see dinosaurs that lived 140 million years ago.

  _____ The clock in the time machine is set 140 million years ago.

2. What is the main idea about dinosaurs in paragraph two?

  _____ Finding dinosaurs can be fun.

  __X__ Finding dinosaurs can be dangerous.

3. What is the main reason Anna and Dr. Valdez jump back into their machine?

  _____ They have seen enough dinosaurs.

  __X__ The Stegosaurus looks unfriendly.

4. What is a good title for this story?

  __X__ A Close Call   _____ Time Travel

60

All About Gators

Directions: Read the paragraphs and write the answer to each question in a complete sentence.

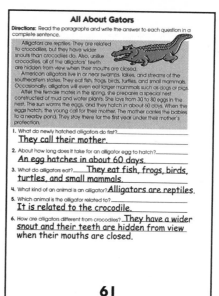

Alligators are reptiles. They are related to crocodiles, but they have wider snouts than crocodiles do. Also, unlike crocodiles, all of the alligators' teeth are hidden from view when their mouths are closed.

American alligators live in or near swamps, lakes, and streams of the southeastern states. They eat fish, frogs, birds, turtles, and small mammals. Occasionally, alligators will even eat larger mammals such as dogs or pigs.

After the female mates in the spring, she prepares a special nest constructed of mud and water plants. She lays from 30 to 80 eggs in the nest. The sun warms the eggs, and they hatch in about 60 days. When the eggs hatch, the young call for their mother. The mother carries the babies to a nearby pond. They stay there for the first year under their mother's protection.

1. What do newly hatched alligators do first? **They call their mother.**

2. About how long does it take for an alligator egg to hatch? **An egg hatches in about 60 days.**

3. What do alligators eat? **They eat fish, frogs, birds, turtles, and small mammals.**

4. What kind of an animal is an alligator? **Alligators are reptiles.**

5. Which animal is the alligator related to? **It is related to the crocodile.**

6. How are alligators different from crocodiles? **They have a wider snout and their teeth are hidden from view when their mouths are closed.**

61

Worth More Than Words

A **conclusion** is a decision you make after thinking about information you have been given. Often, you can judge details in a picture to help you form a conclusion.

Directions: Write an **X** in the box next to each conclusion that makes sense.

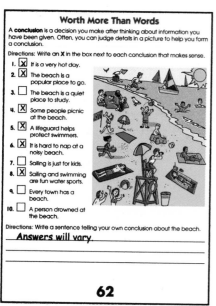

1. [X] It is a very hot day.
2. [X] The beach is a popular place to go.
3. [ ] The beach is a quiet place to study.
4. [X] Some people picnic at the beach.
5. [X] A lifeguard helps protect swimmers.
6. [X] It is hard to nap on a noisy beach.
7. [ ] Sailing is just for kids.
8. [X] Sailing and swimming are fun water sports.
9. [ ] Every town has a beach.
10. [ ] A person drowned at the beach.

Directions: Write a sentence telling your own conclusion about the beach.

Answers will vary. _____

_____

62

Judging a Book by Its Cover

When you use **critical thinking**, often you are using the information you have and your experiences to make a judgment.

Directions: Read the book titles. Write two facts or kinds of information you would expect to find in each book.

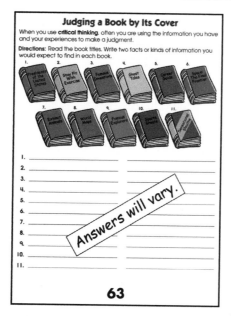

1. _____
2. _____
3. _____
4. _____
5. _____
6. _____
7. _____
8. _____
9. _____
10. _____
11. _____

Answers will vary.

63

If . . . Then

Directions: Underline the **cause** with red and the **effect** with blue.

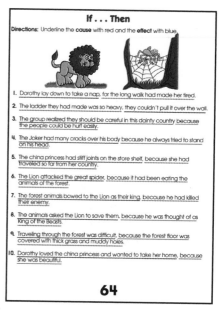

1. Dorothy lay down to take a nap, for the long walk had made her tired.

2. The ladder they had made was so heavy, they couldn't pull it over the wall.

3. The group realized they should be careful in this dainty country because the people could be hurt easily.

4. The Joker had many cracks over his body because he always tried to stand on his head.

5. The china princess had stiff joints on the store shelf, because she had traveled so far from her country.

6. The Lion attacked the great spider, because it had been eating the animals of the forest.

7. The forest animals bowed to the Lion as their king, because he had killed their enemy.

8. The animals asked the Lion to save them, because he was thought of as King of the Beasts.

9. Traveling through the forest was difficult, because the forest floor was covered with thick grass and muddy holes.

10. Dorothy loved the china princess and wanted to take her home, because she was beautiful.

64

What's Next?

Directions: Write two sentences that predict different possible outcomes.

The smoke from the oven rose in the air toward the smoke detector.

1. _____
2. _____

The crowd cheered wildly as the football player ran toward the goal line.

1. _____
2. _____

Bob and Kelly were on their way to the ___ realized she had left her money at home.

1. _____
2. _____

When Rob ___ ___ tour, he found that the tour had started ten minutes e___

1. _____
2. _____

Just as Sam was to go on stage for the class play, he realized he had forgotten his lines.

1. _____
2. _____

Answers will vary.

65

Extra! Extra! Read All About It!

Newspaper reporters have very important jobs. They have to catch a reader's attention and, at the same time, tell the facts.

Newspaper reporters write their stories by answering the questions **who, what, where, when, why,** and **how.**

Directions: Think about a book you have just read and answer the questions below.

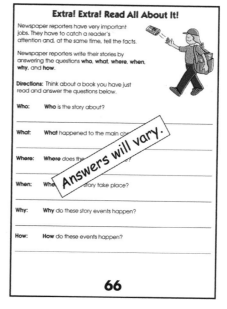

Who: Who is the story about?
_____

What: What happened to the main ch___
_____

Where: Where does the ___
_____

When: Whe___ ___ story take place?
_____

Why: Why do these story events happen?
_____

How: How do these events happen?
_____

Answers will vary.

66

Extra! Extra! Read All About It! cont.

Directions: Use your answers on the previous page to write a newspaper article about the book you read.

BIG CITY TIMES

(Write a catchy title for your article.)

Answers will vary.

67

Write Your Own Story

You may want to create a story just for fun! Once you have chosen the kind of story you want to write, you should brainstorm for ideas. But remember, a good story should have a beginning, a middle, and an end. You can use an outline to organize your ideas.

Directions: Write your ideas for a story to complete this outline.

Kind of Story (mystery, adventure, etc.) _____

I. Setting (where and when the story takes place)

  A. Where _____ Description _____

  B. When _____

II. Characters (people in the story)

  A. Name _____

  B. Name _____

  C. Name _____ Description _____

  D. Name _____ Description _____

III. Plot (events of the story) List main events in order.

  A. _____

  B. _____

  C. _____

  D. _____

Answers will vary.

68

Right in Between

Guide words tell you the first and last word that appears on a dictionary page. The **entry word** you are looking for will appear on a page if it comes between the guide words in alphabetical order.

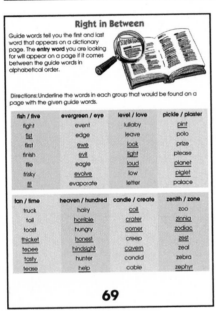

Directions: Underline the words in each group that would be found on a page with the given guide words.

fish / five	evergreen / eye	level / love	pickle / plaster
fight	event	lullaby	pint
fist	edge	leave	polo
first	ewe	look	prize
finish	evil	light	please
file	eagle	loud	planet
frisky	evolve	low	piglet
fit	evaporate	letter	palace

tan / time	heaven / hundred	candle / create	zenith / zone
truck	hairy	coil	zoo
tail	horrible	crater	zinnia
toast	hungry	corner	zodiac
thicket	honest	creep	zest
tepee	hindsight	cavern	zeal
tasty	hunter	candid	zebra
tease	help	cable	zephyr

69

Between the Goalposts

Directions: Circle each football word that would appear alphabetically between each pair of guide words.

heart – hooray: huddle, halfback, **hike**, handoff, **helmet**, holding

penalty – pompom: pass, punt, pads, **play**, **pennant**, practice

table – track: **tackle**, **touchdown**, team, **trap**, trophy, **tailback**

back – blitz: bowl, **backfield**, **band**, **block**, bleacher, **ball**

score – stadium: safety, sweep, sack, **second**, **screen**, **snap**

camera – college: **coach**, **chalk**, **center**, **champion**, corner, **catch**

first – fullback: field, **flanker**, **football**, **fumble**, **flag**, **first**

gallop – grill: **guard**, **grass**, **goal**, **game**, **gridiron**, gain

70
